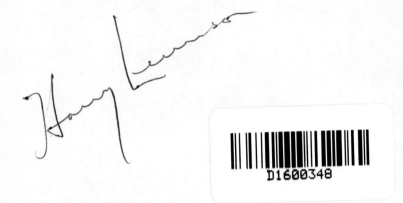

Men, Management,
and Mental Health

Men, Management, and Mental Health

HARRY LEVINSON

CHARLTON R. PRICE

KENNETH J. MUNDEN

HAROLD J. MANDL

CHARLES M. SOLLEY

HARVARD UNIVERSITY PRESS
Cambridge, Massachusetts
1962

Library of Congress Catalog Card No. 62–19218

Printed in the United States of America

To
The Men and Women of Midland —
Our Collaborators

PREFACE

Recent advances in psychiatric research and treatment give growing hope that ways of preventing mental illness may be found. Clinicians and social scientists have collaborated in mapping the incidence and prevalence of mental illness in various cultures, social classes, and geographical areas. Other studies have shown how the mental hospital milieu influences the course of the patient's recovery. These and other investigations indicate that if we are to learn how mental illness can be averted, the relationships between the person and his environment must be more fully understood.

One important aspect of the environment is work experience. In our culture, most people who work full time spend approximately half of their waking hours on the job. For large numbers of adults work experience means membership in an organization, which may continue over many years. A person in a company is affected by the crosscurrents of organizational life, and by the economic fate of the organization. Sometimes he is in conflict with the organization because of demands the company makes on him and those he makes on the company.

Thus, much of how a person feels about himself and the world around him derives from his experiences while earning a living. But because the work environment involves more than a person's individual job assignment, or immediate work group, a concern with mental health in work situations must take into account the context within which these work situations are established, the organization of business and industry.

Accordingly, when The Menninger Foundation began considering what might be done to prevent mental illness, the ex-

perience of people in business and industrial organizations became an appropriate concern. A somewhat similar concern with
human relations in the work place had been evident for some
years among many people in management, industrial medicine,
organized labor, and the social sciences. Although some have
conceived of "human relations" solely as a managerial technique,
there has been a belief that efforts to foster better mental health
through improved industrial human relations are a social responsibility which must be met, along with a realization that work
experience has significant but as yet inadequately understood
effects upon mental health.

So far as the issue of prevention of mental illness is concerned,
many are now convinced that early treatment, such as psychological first-aid programs in the military services and in some
industrial plants, is a step toward but not an adequate substitute
for other kinds of preventive efforts which might be evolved.
Furthermore, organizations cannot escape the problems of mental
illness by trying to "weed out" those who are likely to break
down, since every person may become ill under some kinds or
degrees of stress.

In 1954, The Menninger Foundation undertook a survey of
the kinds of mental health problems which occur in industry
and what was being done about them. The senior author of
this volume visited many companies to observe their personnel
management practices; talked with occupational physicians, industrial psychologists, and investigators in academic research
centers; studied human relations programs, union-sponsored
counseling services, management development programs and
similar activities, and began to sample the literature in the various specialized fields related to mental health in industry. From
this 1954 survey came the decision that if financial support could
be secured, The Menninger Foundation should establish an
industrial mental health program. In 1955 a grant from the
Rockefeller Brothers Fund made this plan a reality. A Division
of Industrial Mental Health was formed.

Many useful surveys of current practices in industrial health and human relations were already available, and our own preliminary work (27) had made it possible to summarize much of this growing body of information. We decided that a careful, exploratory investigation of work experience in one organization, complementing what others had been learning and reporting in the literature, would be our first step.

Our initial study, we reasoned, should be undertaken in an organization large enough and diversified enough to include a variety of activities and situations which could be studied comparatively. It should be an organization similar to other businesses in its structure and activities, so that the conclusions that we might reach could be generalized and applied in other work situations. Finally, because we sought at this early stage in our work to raise new questions and problems for further research, rather than to test hypotheses or to become consultants on industrial mental health, we needed to study in an organization which was willing to collaborate with us without expecting to receive findings which would be of direct benefit to the organization itself. All of these conditions were fulfilled, to our good fortune, in the Midland Utilities Company. The actual name of the company and all names of persons and places connected with it which are mentioned in this book have been changed. Some aspects of examples cited have been altered to ensure anonymity.

We approached the problem of relationships between work and mental health from a background of clinical experience in a psychiatric setting. This experience led to a number of specific decisions about the way in which the study would be done. Our team included both clinicians and social scientists, just as the diagnostic or therapeutic team in the clinical settings draws upon various professional skills. Furthermore, we directed our primary attention to people and their individual functioning rather than to the organization as an operating system — its efficiency or its profitability. We started with the raw material of experience, as we could learn about it through observation and interview methods.

Our encounters with the people in the organization led to our greater understanding of the conditions under which various kinds of experiences at work, positive or negative with respect to mental health, are likely to occur. We believe that these encounters enabled the people at Midland to share their experiences with us more freely than if more formal research methods had been used.

To repeat: In this study we are not concerned with assessing the functioning of the Midland Company as an organization. It would not be possible, either from the body of our data or from that portion of it reported in this volume, to evaluate the adequacy of Midland from an economic, technical, administrative, or even mental health point of view. Our purpose in this study is much more limited. It is to understand some of the effects of work experiences on mental health.

In any study of real-life behavior (as opposed to social science or clinical investigations under experimental conditions) a large amount of information about individual personalities as well as particular group and organizational situations becomes available. The interpretations we were able to make were based on evidence from many sources. But to report all of the supporting evidence would violate the spirit of confidentiality and trust in which the information was made available. Therefore, in fairness to those who helped us to learn, much of our data cannot be reported here and at some points the reader may have to take our word for the validity of our assertions.

While we cannot give the reader all of the evidence for our conclusions which he might wish to have, we can and do outline the major factors which we believe must be taken into account for an understanding of any given work situation from a mental health point of view. These general remarks will constitute our interpretations throughout the book. We attempt to state these interpretations in a way which should be of interest to those

with management responsibility in organizations, to others who
are studying work behavior and human relations in industry,
and to clinicians who may wish to make greater use of data
on work experience in their diagnosis, treatment, or rehabilitation of psychiatric patients.

This, then, is an exploratory study. It describes and interprets
some of the experiences that people at work in one industrial
organization undergo; many of these we saw but most were
reported. This study is concerned with how these experiences
affect the mental health of these people. We look upon mental
health as being related primarily to how a person feels about
himself, about people, about the world around him and his place
in it, and about his experiences while earning a living for himself and those who depend on him.

As a contribution toward the development of a preventive
psychiatry, this study provides another avenue for understanding
the psychological relationship of a man and the organization in
which he works. It offers some concepts for systematizing the
experiences of work in an organization and relating them to
mental health. Out of this study have come some suggested ways
in which management, by managerial actions, can contribute
to mental health. Ultimately, we hope to be able to specify a
wide range of activities which management can undertake to
foster mental health.

We feel that this study makes a contribution in several additional respects:

1. It emphasizes the mental health implications which exist in
   the relationship between the man and his company;
2. It offers some suggestions about ways of counteracting the
   impersonalizing effects of company mergers and growth;
3. It elaborates some ideas about human relations in industry
   which help make the general term "human relations" more
   specific;
4. It serves as a provocation for any manager or executive to

examine his own role and the relationship of what he does
to the mental health of his subordinates.

We suggest that the reader will find this book most useful if
he juxtaposes each example with one from his own experience.
If he will then look into his own example for the kinds of
processes we discuss, he will have some way of judging the usefulness of our observations in terms of his own experience. He
will also come to his own recognition of some of the inadequacies
and limitations of our observations and raise some important
questions of his own.

We want to emphasize particularly the importance of viewing
experience as a continuous process so that one can think of people not in an oversimplified fashion as aggressive or passive,
motivated or lethargic, introverted or extroverted, but as responding to a complex of internal and external forces, many of
which can be abstracted and understood as one observes people
at work. The reader who seeks simple sequential answers in
recipe fashion will be disappointed. There are no prescriptions
here. There are, however, some ways of thinking about the
meaning of the work experience and the mental health of people
in business organizations.

ACKNOWLEDGMENTS

As is always true in a collaborative undertaking such as this,
we have many specific reasons to be grateful to a large number
of people who have helped us at every stage of our work.

Warren Bennis, G. T. Bowden, Seward Hiltner, William C.
Menninger, Karl Menninger, Gardner Murphy, and Edward G.
Nelson critically reviewed the entire manuscript. Their many
thoughtful comments contributed much to the final form these
chapters took, although we ourselves are responsible for how we
used their suggestions.

Carter Umbarger and Robert McKay each spent a summer

with us as research assistants, and Seymour Liss for a longer period.

Mrs. Yvonne Lambott, Mrs. Marilyn Hamman, Mrs. Ruth Kurz, Mrs. Margery Wiebe, Mrs. Jean Senecal, and Mrs. Judith Jackson, spent untold hours typing interviews, diaries, and manuscript. Mrs. Mary D. Lee and Nelson Antrim Crawford reviewed the manuscript in detail and made innumerable editorial improvements. Thomas D. Ketchum made additional editorial comments.

The work of the Division of Industrial Mental Health of The Menninger Foundation, including the study reported here and the methods manual, *Interdisciplinary Research on Work and Mental Health: A Point of View and a Method* (Topeka, The Menninger Foundation, 1961), has been supported at various times during the past seven years by the Rockefeller Brothers Fund, the International Harvester Foundation, the Sears Roebuck Foundation, the Fluor Foundation, the Northwest Paper Foundation, the Marathon Oil Foundation, Inc., the Fleischmann Foundation, the General Electric Foundation, the General Foods Corporation, Owen-Illinois, the Levinson Foundation, the Tektronix Foundation, Dr. Alan McLean, the California Portland Cement Company, the Consolidated Natural Gas Company, the American Telephone and Telegraph Company, and the Connecticut Mutual Life Insurance Company.

Our colleague, Howard V. Perlmutter, participated in many discussions with us and offered numerous ideas as we prepared the manuscript. The creative editorial work of Mrs. Helen Friend is so much a part of this book that for all practical purposes she is a collaborator in the writing.

Drs. William C. Menninger and Karl A. Menninger, by encouragement, support, guidance, and patience not only made it possible for this study to come to fruition, but, more importantly, anticipated the need for concern with mental health in industry. Their interest led to the organization of a Division of Industrial Mental Health in The Menninger Foundation. We are indebted also to our professional colleagues of The Menninger Foundation, always ready to help, who stimulated our thinking and whose point of view gave us the tools with which to start our search. We are particularly indebted to Lester T. Roach, Executive Secretary, and Irving Sheffel, Comptroller, for consultation, guidance in the field of management, and administrative support for this project.

Our greatest debt, of course, is to the management and employees of Midland, and particularly to its chief executive officer. They gave us hours upon hours of their time, not only during the field work, but after it as well. Despite the pressures of their own work, including the emergencies with which people in any public utility company must deal frequently, they were constantly available to us. Though their contribution to this study was made at considerable cost in time and inconvenience, they neither asked nor received anything in return. To let strangers enter into one's business for a period of years, for their purposes, without knowing what they were learning until the manuscript was prepared, required considerable conviction and forbearance. To encourage them continuously and be supportive to them took extraordinary confidence and faith. Every researcher and businessman will appreciate how deeply indebted we are.

Finally, we owe deep thanks to our wives, whose patience was often sorely tried as we spent week after week in the field and night after night preoccupied with data and manuscript. Without their confidence and affection the task would indeed have been far more difficult.

The Authors

Contents

Persons can be conceived as taking some particular stance toward the historical, supra-personal, past. They will be memorializing it, rejecting it, recreating it, cashing in on it, escaping, or in flight from it; these are but a few of the countless possibilities. Personal styles are built around such possibilities, and entire series of personal acts may be viewed as strategies in rejecting, escaping, recapturing, and the like. A man may write a book, marry a woman, or build an organization for such ends. When we interview persons we catch them during some temporal cross section in the building or transforming of styles that lead to history; this is one important way to regard the contents of interviews and conversations.

> Anselm L. Strauss, *Mirrors and Masks*. Glencoe, Ill., The Free Press, 1959, p. 169.

**Men, Management,
and Mental Health**

CHAPTER I

MIDLAND

O<small>N</small> September 19, 1957, a Midland Utilities pipeline crew pulled up at a new gas well and began unloading pipe and equipment, getting ready to tie the well into the company's transmission line. A raw wind was blowing. The crew worked fast to keep warm and finish the job before dark. The district superintendent had dropped by to see how they were getting along.

Just as the trenching machine began to bite into the prairie soil, a message came in over the short-wave radio. The crew foreman and superintendent listened intently for a few seconds, and then shouted to the rest of the crew to load up again. A major line break had occurred some 50 miles away.

In a few minutes the trucks were rolling, with the district superintendent's car in the lead. As the trucks raced to the area of the break, the radio messages continued giving the superintendent more details on the emergency.

Some miles down the highway, one truck was detoured to a county road where it stopped beside a bypass valve. The two men in the truck jumped out and switched the gas flow to an undamaged parallel line. They stayed at the valve to close off the flow entirely if the second line should also fail. The foreman went on to the warehouse to pick up couplings and two men who were welders.

The superintendent and the rest of the crew rushed on to the break. Finally they came to a stop beside two parked cars in a wet stretch of bottomland beside a levee. Near the cars stood the general pipeline superintendent, the manager of Midland operations in a nearby town, and several pipeliners from another crew.

The whole group sloshed through the field and climbed up on the levee to survey the situation.

Out in the middle of the broad shallow river channel, water was still bubbling as some gas continued to escape from the pipe. Apparently high water from heavy rains had burrowed beneath two parallel high-pressure lines which were buried in the river bed. The combined force of the current and the pressure of the gas inside the lines (about 350 pounds per square inch at this time of year) had snapped a joint in one of the pipes. There had been a tremendous explosion, so loud that a two-man crew working four miles below the break had heard it and looked up to see the column of water. They had immediately cut over the bypass valve to the north of the explosion, just as the incoming transmission men had cut over the valve to the south.

The general superintendent looked at the river. "Unless that damn water goes down, we can't fix the pipe. I hope to hell that other line doesn't blow," he said.

The district superintendent suggested, and the general superintendent agreed, that the best thing to do was to try to sandbag the remaining line and hope that it would hold.

But this would be no simple task. In order to sandbag the pipe, the crew needed a boat to get to a nearby sandbar and some burlap sacks to fill when they got there. They would also need some rubber boots, because their own boots were back at the pipeline warehouse which they had left early that morning.

But by this time, other trucks and men had arrived — the trailer truck from the field, the foreman and two welders, and the standby crew from the local division. The general superintendent told them where to unload their equipment. He then set out for town to find a boat and the burlap bags. He found one store which had a new boat and motor. Nothing else was available. Asking to use the boat, the superintendent explained the situation to the store owner, "I'm from Midland. We'll make good on any damage to the boat. We have an emergency out here. A line blew."

Outside the boat store the superintendent paused for a moment. Suddenly, for the first time, he recognized that he had been followed by a researcher who had been with the crew all along. "I thought you fellows were just going to talk to us in the office," he said incredulously. He chuckled, slapped his companion on the back, and walked to his car.

Back at the river the men waited for the superintendent to return. The equipment was ready to go, but nothing further could be done until the boat arrived. They occupied their time with horseplay. Several of the men began telling the crew foreman that he ought to get some whiskey to ward off the cold and damp. The foreman razzed them back. Later, when the superintendent appeared with the boat, the men gathered around him for their instructions. And so began the slow, nasty, and dangerous task of assuring a continued flow of gas to Midland's customers.

The Men Speak

Some weeks later the researcher who had witnessed the line break spent another day with the same crew. This time there was more opportunity to talk with the men about their everyday work experience.

The driver of the big trailer truck used to haul pipe and machinery, one of the younger and newer members of the crew, talked about the variety of things that had to be done in his job:

I like to work on the truck but these long hauls can get pretty damn tiresome. A few weeks back we didn't do nothing but move pipe for days at a time. It's good to get out and get a little exercise work, like today when we're tieing in this well. I like the idea of not sitting in one spot. That explosion you saw — that was a good deal. You never know what the hell you're going to do when you get up and go in in the morning. I kinda like to mess with the machinery. I don't think it hurts a man to know a little about all these jobs on the crew.

Some days, of course, go better than others. A young welder's helper only three years with the crew, mentioned that:

I've seen the guys so damn cold that you couldn't hardly breathe and they were just as happy as anything. Other days it would be a nice day and they'd just get mad, so mad they might hurt themselves. Mostly the feeling builds up right there at the warehouse of a morning. I don't know how it works but that's what it is.

He pointed out that everyone who joins the crew has to go through an initiation. They are "worked over" by the older hands before they are accepted as a member of the group:

Everybody does a lot of razzing, of course. When you first come on the crew, they look at you kinda funny if you can't take it. We only had one guy who couldn't take the razzing. He only stayed a month or so. I guess he thought he was too good to work out here. I guess it was okay that he went away.

But there was more in the relationship among the crew members than razzing. The youngest member of the crew put it this way:

I like my relations with a guy on this crew here. You can get a lot of work done just joking along. On that explosion you saw, everything went swell. We joked all night with each other even though we were in a hell of a bind. That's what happens. You can come down in the morning and feel tired and blue and you forget about your troubles after joking around on the crew a little bit.

The crew foreman had a weatherbeaten look. His battered hunting cap and worn shirt, trousers, and poplin jacket were splattered with rustproofing pipe paint. He explained that he had spent all his working life in the gas fields, yet wondered why he had chosen this kind of work and then stayed with it so long:

This is my life, right here . . . I don't know why you follow a line like this. It's fantastic or whatever you want to call it. I brought gas to this part of the country.

The gas crew leads a roving life. The foreman said that lately he and his men had been within driving distance of their homes in town each night more often than not. Still, the work site may be anywhere within an area of hundreds of square miles, and they go to a different place almost every day:

We do a lot of moving around on this job. Some of these wells don't last three months. You've got to pick up the pipe and move it somewhere else.

He then told how he tries to run the crew:

The main thing is to keep them on the go all the time. Each one has to do his part. He has to show that he wants something besides just being out there. I don't like to have to tell a man to pick up a shovel and move that dirt. I like them to look at the job and go ahead without me dictating. This is a good bunch of boys. They all know what to do.

In the foreman's view, there is more to running a crew than just seeing that the job gets done:

Running a group of men is just like you're trying to raise a family. If you must jump a man and eat him out for something wrong, you can make it worse. You don't get up and throw your voice around. A foreman's got to bite his tongue and overlook things a lot of times. Being a foreman over a bunch of men is not all grapes, I can tell you. Lots of times in this pipeline work you're into a lot of stuff that you don't like — into mud up to your hind end, or out in the cold in a freeze up on a line.

He then talked about the company itself, and his relationship to the company and management.

It takes us guys to make them guys [management]. You've got to have cooperation on both sides. You've got to give and take. Unless we do our job, they don't look very good.

The Work Environment

This crew was one of many in the Midland Company whom we observed and to whom we talked. Our interest in the relationships between work experience and mental health took us to the men of the pipeline crew and to hundreds of others working in various parts of the Midland organization, not only in gas transmission operations but on the electric service, in power plants, in warehouses and offices. We had to learn first-hand what kinds of experiences people in various parts of the company were likely to have in the course of a day's work. Thus we spent many weeks on the job with crews in the field and with clerks, supervisors and management in local company offices. Additional hours were spent with executives at Midland headquarters.

The company was divided into twelve geographical divisions. Eight of these provided gas and electric services, two provided electric service only, and two provided gas service only. In addition to the allocation of responsibility according to geographical areas, there were lines of communication and control from the headquarters level down to gas and electric operations in each of the local areas. The various work activities at Midland, and the connections between them, are outlined in the accompanying chart, "The Pattern of Operations at Midland."

For the men of the pipeline crew and for other gas and electric field crews, the day's work is out-of-doors, often miles away from others in the company or the home town. Activities change in such groups from day to day and even from hour to hour as the crew moves from one job to another, or responds to an emergency. Most crews are free to set their own work pace and to divide up among themselves the total work assignment, which is given to the foreman before the crew leaves the warehouse at the beginning of the day.

A man on the line, as the members of the pipeline crew pointed out, has to be able to "take it." "It" includes not only razzing from fellow crew members but, more importantly, sustained performance in emergencies, often for long hours and in severe weather. Physical demands are comparatively heavy: climbing, lifting, digging, using tools and power equipment. "But if you're under 45 or 50," a veteran line foreman said, "the best job in the company is to be out there climbing the poles from eight to five."

The people on the line see office life as quite different from theirs; as one of them put it, "There's a lot of writing, and you have to mix with the management." In the office, the company meets Main Street. Many customers go there to request service and to pay their bills. In the larger towns, the office is the head-

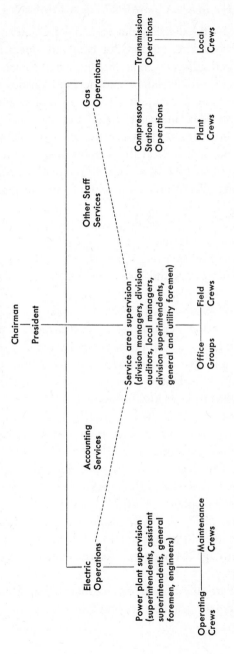

THE PATTERN OF OPERATIONS AT MIDLAND
(A schematic view)

Chairman

President

Electric Operations — Accounting Services — Other Staff Services — Gas Operations

Power plant supervision (superintendents, assistant superintendents, general foremen, engineers)

Operating Crews — Maintenance Crews

Service area supervision (division managers, division auditors, local managers, division superintendents, general and utility foremen)

Office Groups — Field Crews

Compressor Station Operations — Transmission Operations

Plant Crews

Local Crews

quarters for the division manager, the division engineer, and their staffs, who are responsible for company operations in the community and adjacent areas. In the office women take orders and payments from customers, and perform various bookkeeping operations under the supervision of a division auditor, sometimes called the office manager. In all but the smallest communities, there is little contact between the office people and the crewmen who spend their time at the warehouse or on the trucks.

Still another type of work environment at Midland is found in the plants. There are a number of electric generating stations, some large and new, some older, smaller, and relatively obsolescent. There are also compressor stations, spaced along the many miles of transmission pipeline to maintain gas pressure. Directions from headquarters units tell people in the stations when to place compressors and generators on the line to meet the changing load demands.

The plants are usually located in open country, and the people working within them are somewhat isolated from others in the company and the customers. While customers may have seen the crews, and have business with the local offices, few have seen the inside of a plant.

The power plants are characterized by the roar of burning fuel which creates steam in the massive boilers. The steam, in turn, drives large generators which hum continuously. In the compressor stations, giant pistons move horizontally, each at a different rhythm. The pounding of the pistons mingles with the hiss of gas under high pressure in the pipes above and beneath the floor. In both kinds of plants, work goes on around the clock, as men on successive shifts patrol the miles of pipe, take readings on the performance of the machines, keep floors and equipment spotless, and guard against dangerous consequences of human or mechanical error.

There are still other work environments at Midland: the county fair, where a home economist might demonstrate the use of home appliances fueled by the company's products; the warehouse, where the crew trucks depart each morning and return at night, while testing of meters, equipment, and storeroom work goes on through the day; a city council meeting, where a local manager might negotiate a renewal of the company's franchise to operate in the community.

Thus daily work experience at Midland takes place, as in any company, within a particular kind of work environment. This environment includes work associates as well as those who make plans and decisions at a distant company office. The formal structure of authority is a part of it. So is the daily give-and-take of work activity in offices, along country roads or city streets, and around the clock in the power plant or compressor station.

The Growth of Midland

The original Midland company had been organized soon after World War I as one subsidiary of a holding company which owned and operated public utilities in several midwestern states, mostly in urban areas. One of these areas, the city of Shaw and its environs, had a growing demand for electric power, and the first responsibility of the subsidiary was to construct and operate a new plant to provide additional capacity. Through the decade before World War II, Midland extended its operations from the original territory in and around Shaw to many other towns, and acquired gas as well as electric properties.

Much of this growth was made possible when federal legislation required the dissolution in the 1930's of holding companies, including that which controlled Midland and similar firms. With holding company control removed, some of the former subsidiaries were in difficult circumstances. A number of them were inadequately capitalized or served unprofitable markets, and during the depression all had been losing revenue. But Midland was in a stronger position than most. It had promising market prospects, experienced management, and a larger staff than many of the neighboring companies. All of these factors made it possible for the Midland organization to acquire many of the other former holding company subsidiaries.

In the course of growth and change, every organization develops a distinctive character, evident both to its members and to those outsiders who may come in contact with its people and activities. References to a company's "personality" or "way of doing things" take account of this feature of organizations. This relatively diffuse aspect of organizational life includes the goals and values which the organization has adopted in the course of its history. These public expressions of organizational purpose, like the physical and social surroundings on the job, are another important feature of the work environment, since on-the-job behavior is influenced by the purposes and values which the organization as a whole is designed to pursue.

Service, for example, was one such central value at Midland. It found formal expression in the company trade-mark, its employee publications, and its advertising. It was personalized in the expressed belief of executives that effective public relations depended more upon the quality of service rendered by individual employees in their relationships with customers, than upon press releases and staff activities at the headquarters level.

Another central value at Midland was the commitment to free enterprise principles in the utility business. As all privately owned utilities had done for many years, Midland protested against efforts by government, particularly at the federal level, to compete in this field.

A third central value was Midland as a good neighbor. Midland people were encouraged to carry their share of community responsibilities. Midland trucks would stop on the highway so the men might help a motorist change a tire. Midland executives took important roles in community-wide projects.

In postwar years, Midland was faced with the need to expand its facilities rapidly to meet mounting demands for both gas and electric services. The pressure for growth was particularly heavy on the electrical side of the business. There were personnel short-ages in prospect, particularly in middle management ranks. Many division managers and senior field supervisors were nearing re-tirement age, and there were few ready to step in as replacements. Some key jobs had to be filled from outside the company.

Thus at the time of the study Midland had been in existence for more than a generation. It had grown from a service area around one community to a territory covering thousands of square miles and hundreds of towns. It employed almost two thousand people in the various types of work locations already described. It was going through a number of changes in personnel and op-erations. These circumstances add another dimension to the work situation — memories of the past and expectations of the future, which differed for people at different levels.

Top management people, speaking of the past (and of the fu-ture), viewed Midland's past as a story of increasing autonomy. They identified themselves with this movement. One top manage-ment executive, for example, explained how he had worked to build an organization from the parts left by the dissolution of the holding companies. These efforts had included acquiring new properties and building a management force competent enough to operate the properties being acquired. All of this experience was viewed as the core of his personal achievement.

Most of the middle management group had been in the smaller, merged companies, and many still lived with vivid memories of the merged companies though in some cases the mergers had oc-curred 20 years before. In their interviews, middle management dwelt heavily on changes in leadership, particularly on the grow-ing distance between themselves and top management. They spoke also of greater formalization of procedures within the grow-ing organization and the consequent decreasing opportunity for giving personal service to customers. The future would inevitably bring increasing refinement of administrative techniques with greater emphasis on specialized procedures (for example, cen-tralized machine bookkeeping) and relationships with headquarters staff specialists in such areas as new business, accounting, and engineering, rather than with top management itself.

Still another view of the company's past came from many people at the field level. Here, the emphasis was on increasing security provided by the company as a company. Many had been with the company through the depression and viewed themselves as fortunate compared to their friends. Others had experienced considerable deprivation during the depression, and still others had come to the company after leaving or losing marginal farms. Security had an especially poignant meaning for these people. Security included not only economic guarantees, but also better tools, easier work, greater safety and increasing community prestige, all of which they had experienced and associated with opportunities afforded them in the company. They anticipated the continued growth of demands for utility services and as a result looked toward a future of economic stability. Many had bought stock in the company.

The psychological effects of the entire work environment, present realities as well as views of the past and future, will become apparent in the subsequent chapters.

CHAPTER II

APPROACH

AT the beginning of the previous chapter, we described an event in the field with a Midland work crew and some additional aspects of their work experience we learned about in talking with the men. Such experiences are characteristic for many people in Midland Utilities. We have sketched some of the settings in which Midland people work, how the job is organized, as well as the history and the values of the organization. How were we to abstract from data like these, ideas and hypotheses which would be helpful in developing knowledge that could be used to foster mental health in work situations?

We might have interpreted work experiences in Midland in many different ways. "It takes us guys to make them guys," the foreman of the gas transmission crew had said, speaking of management. His further comments and those of all of the others with whom we talked, together with our observations, would have enabled us to analyze the impact of organizational norms on individual motivation and behavior. Such is the focal point for several studies by Chris Argyris (1, 2).

On the job with a transmission crew, we saw that the district superintendent dropped by to observe their work. In the emergency, the general superintendent appeared on the scene, as did other company officials. On another visit with the crew, we noted the foreman's mode of supervision, and he expressed his supervisory philosophy in an interview. The men had spoken of what they liked or did not like about their supervision.

Peer relationships were also discussed. "I've seen the guys so damned cold that you couldn't hardly breathe and they were just as happy as anything" the welder's helper had told us. "Everyone takes a lot of razzing," he added. "You can get a lot of work done just joking along," a crew man said. The socializing pattern of the men, reflected in these quotations, provided the raw data from which generalizations could be abstracted about the behavior of small groups and these could then be related to qualities of supervision. Researchers at the University of Michigan (18) and elsewhere have done precisely this type of analysis.

The work itself might have been a focus of study. The gas crew *unloaded pipe* in a raw wind. It *used a trenching machine.* The men *rode to their jobs* over an area of many square miles. They *turned valves, stood by* for further orders. They were to *fill bags with sand* and *place the bags* in position to support the second gas line, a task which required them to work all night in the cold and mud. Later they would *repair the pipe* which had exploded.

The truck drivers had talked about the monotony of the long hauls, the "exercise work," the unexpected emergency, the opportunity to "mess with machinery." The foreman's clothes were splattered with rustproofing paint, and he referred to the digging which had to be done.

The tasks could be spelled out in detail. Each step of each task had its own requirements. Sometimes the task required that the men work together; sometimes each worked alone. Some jobs were onerous, others pleasant. Perhaps there was not much to learn about digging a ditch, but "messing with machinery" gave a man a chance to learn another phase of the work. The task requirements had something to do with the way the men could relate to each other and with their views of their work lives. Leonard Sayles (28), and others, have studied the relationship of this aspect of the work situation to work behavior.

The men talked about their lives off the job. The foreman indicated there were times when the crews were away from home. In their interviews the men talked about what they did after work, both at home and when they were away. They touched on their family problems and frustrations. "You can come down in the morning and feel tired and blue," the young crew member had said as he opened that avenue for discussion. Our study might have concentrated on the relationship of work life and off-work life. A number of people have devoted considerable attention to off-work activities (7, 21, 30).

We did not concentrate on any of these levels nor did we single out dimensions of work experience which could be measured and correlated with each other. We were not ready to make abstractions before we became intimately acquainted with the phenomena we were studying. Furthermore, our concern was with mental health. At the time of the field work we had not yet developed a criterion of mental health. We had no way of saying what it was for our study purposes. Obviously, we could not then say what aspects of work would have a bearing on it.

We assumed, however, that whatever criterion we developed would have two characteristics. First, it would touch upon the many different aspects of work life which had been studied in depth by others for other research purposes. Second, it would have to do particularly with *people's feelings* about themselves and their life situations. Clinical experience had already demonstrated the role of emotions in precipitating mental illness. If our ultimate interest was in learning about possible ways of preventing illness, we also would necessarily be concerned with the emotional significance of events and circumstances in the work situation. Our methods therefore were directed to obtaining as much information as possible from people at Midland about how they saw and felt about their work lives.

We reasoned that if we conducted relatively unstructured interviews in which only a few questions might be asked to stimulate discussion, people would be free to discuss their work situations as they saw them. If we were to interview them at their work, and to record their remarks and our observations while we were there, we might understand the interview content better. Genuine interest on our part, demonstrated by being with them at their work regardless of weather or potential danger, was likely to lead to more useful information about their feelings than we might expect by asking them to complete a questionnaire (34). The pleasant surprise of the general superintendent when he found the researcher with the gas transmission crew, was echoed repeatedly by most of the people to whom we talked.

To the question, "How do you know that they would tell you the truth, and to what extent were the topics they discussed actually the most important ones to them?" there is only one reply. As we told one of the employees who asked this question in an orientation meeting, "We won't know whether you are telling the truth. But then, we will not be considering your interview alone. We will be weighing what many people have said."

We depend then on validation by consensus. Eight hundred seventy-four people were interviewed in many different parts of the company, by three different interviewers who came from different scientific disciplines: clinical psychology (Levinson), psychiatry (Munden), and sociology (Price). The interviews were conducted at different times over a two-year period. A more detailed description of the study method appears in appendix I. The interviewers tried to write down as much of the interview in verbatim form as was possible, during the interview, recording both the interviewee's words and their own. Recorded observations were equally varied. They included various formal aspects of work to which attention has been given by other researchers, as noted previously. If, out of all this variety, there appeared some common concerns, some expressions of common feeling, then we would have reason to accept such concerns as valid.

Inasmuch as this was an exploratory study, an exploratory method was particularly appropriate. If the search is for ideas, then the greatest possible freedom must be given to the idea-seeking process. Researcher and research subject must interact in many different ways so that the former may both observe regularities and develop some notions about why they occur. Such a conception dictates not only what is done in the field, but also how the information gathered is to be analyzed.

The problem of organization and interpretation of the interviews and diary notes was governed also by other considerations already mentioned: the need to draw consensus of feelings from the interviews and to incorporate in any interpretation the observation data as well. The method of choice was a thematic analysis.

After the field work was completed, another clinical psychologist (Mandl) joined the study team, and the four researchers proceeded to analyze the interviews as follows: working in pairs, they read independently all of the interviews obtained in a given company location as well as all of the diary notes related to that location. Diaries included all material other than interviews: observations, comments on research team problems, ideas which came to mind, and incidental information. Each then wrote an interpretation, documented with quotations from interviews and diaries, of what he believed to be the central concerns of people in that situation and how these might be related to what had been observed and reported about the work situation.

The three interviewers, now turned interpreters, would again bring their varying backgrounds to their task. They would now for the first time be drawing inferences from each other's data. The fourth researcher had had no previous contact with the project and could make his interpretations from the interviews alone. As a further precaution against bias, pairings were arranged so that each interpreter had the opportunity to "work with" every other interpreter, although they did not discuss the data or their interpretations until all of the themes had been completed.

When all of the themes had been written, the process of analysis was another extension of the same method. Now the researchers read independently all of the themes, then talked about them together, still with the same question: what were the central concerns and how did they relate to mental health?

Criteria of Mental Health

There is considerable discussion in the literature about the scientific adequacy of the concept of mental health (31). For our purposes we find the concept useful. We therefore developed a working description of mental health. Munden and Solley (32) asked fourteen senior psychiatrists and psychologists of The Menninger Foundation, in private interviews, to describe people whom they had known and whom they regarded to be mentally healthy. From their descriptions we abstracted five aspects of behavior which were characteristic of these people, judged by clinicians to be mentally healthy:

1. *They treated others as individuals.* This means they were not only sensitive to individual differences among people, but also that they were able to establish good relationships with other people despite these differences. Its opposite would be to view other people as impersonal sources of reward or punishment; to view them as if they were in fact the same as parents, relatives, or other figures from the past; or stereotypes or genotypes.

2. *They were flexible under stress.* Dealing with stress flexibly might mean, for example, to suffer the loss of a loved one with grief but not depression. Stress, as defined here, would include both internal and environmental pressures which threaten to disrupt the organized way in which a person customarily behaves.

3. *They obtained gratification from a wide variety of sources:* people, ideas, tasks, interests, values.

4. *They accepted their own capacities and limitations.* This relates to a realistic self-concept, neither overvaluing nor undervaluing one's potentialities. With such a self-concept a person is better able to make full use of the resources available to him.

5. *They were active and productive.* That is, they spontaneously and naturally used their capacities in the interest of their own self-fulfillment and in the service of others. This differed from a neurotically driven need to achieve.

If these aspects of behavior were characteristic of people who were judged to have mental health, then our question became, "How does work experience encourage people to behave in these ways, or, conversely, how does it inhibit them in doing so?" What could our knowledge of life at Midland, now summarized in thematic form, tell us which would bear upon these aspects of behavior?

Central Concerns

Out of study of the themes and extended group discussions, the researchers identified three central concerns. In one way or another, these concerns recurred throughout our data and the preliminary analyses of them: interdependence with the company; the comfort of relationships with fellow employees, superiors, and subordinates; and the experience of change, both in personal life and in the company. These concerns clearly were not unrelated. One or another might be highlighted in various themes. But they were differentiated sufficiently to impress the researchers, and the elaboration of each, as in the subsequent chapters, made it more possible to understand the subtlety of their interaction.

Discussion of the themes revealed two features of these concerns. First, the efforts of people to obtain a satisfactory interdependent relationship with the company, comfortable interpersonal relationships, and to deal with change reasonably well, were reciprocal. Second, people had very strong expectations related to these concerns.

The Reciprocal Process

When people did something, to, for, or in behalf of the company or other people, others in turn responded in some fashion to them. One way of viewing work experience was as the operation of such a reciprocal process.

In the work situation, for example, a person is a member of the organization. The organization has certain minimal conditions and requirements which must be met if he is to remain a member. Similarly, the person demands of the organization minimal guarantees of continuity, financial reward, and other acknowledgments that he is contributing to a larger organizational purpose.

Work life also involves other people and other groups. They demand of the individual that he contribute to the group purposes, that he learn and respond to the ways of behaving which are traditionally acceptable in that group, and that he identify with the group of which he is a member in his dealings with those outside the group. At the same time, the person demands of the group that he be recognized as some *one*, with an individual and unique identity, that he be accepted as a person with a status position and role to play within the group, and that he be given some assurance that the group will survive, for his fortunes are bound up with what happens to the group.

A third aspect of work experience is the task. The task has its own formal requirements and the person brings to the task capacities, interests, and skills which permit him to fulfill these requirements more or less effectively. Thus the reciprocal process, or reciprocation, involves all of the various aspects of work life within an organization. E. Wight Bakke (3) and Alvin Gouldner (12) have given considerable attention to some sociological aspects of the process described here as reciprocation.

Expectations

In addition to reciprocation, an important characteristic of the three central concerns was the expectations which people held about them. As people spoke about their work experiences, directly or tacitly they spoke of expectations — those which they thought were going to be fulfilled, those which had or had not been fulfilled, and those on the basis of which they were operating in the present. Of course, the company, too, had expectations of its people, as expressed in policies and practices, and in varying degrees the people were aware of them.

The frequency with which these expectations seemed to have an almost obligatory quality was impressive to us. As people expressed their expectations, or even where expectations were tacit, it was as if the company or other people were duty-bound to fulfill them. Consideration of this feature of the interviews and themes called to mind Karl Menninger's discussion (25) of intangible aspects of contractual relationships, out of which we evolved the concept of the "psychological contract."

The expectations of both employees and company were then conceived as components of a psychological contract. Such a contract is rarely made formal. It is a much broader conception than the traditional use of the word in industrial relations where it has come to mean the specifics of a written legal agreement between management and labor. The psychological contract is a series of mutual expectations of which the parties to the relationship may not themselves be even dimly aware but which nonetheless govern their relationship to each other. Given this framework, it became evident to us that reciprocation could be understood as the way in which the contract is affirmed, altered, or denied in day-to-day work experience within the organization.

To return to the aspects of behavior characteristic of mental health, we hypothesize that where reciprocation functions well, where the psychological contract is being fulfilled, such aspects of behavior occur in the work situation as a kind of psychological by-product. Put a different way, those events and circumstances which foster the operation of reciprocation in turn facilitate the occurrence of these aspects of behavior. In our discussion of the psychological contract, the central concerns, and later, of reciprocation, we shall illustrate how work experience comes to be related to the mental health of people in an organization.

CHAPTER III

THE UNWRITTEN CONTRACT

The psychological or unwritten contract is a product of mutual expectations. These have two characteristics: (a) They are largely implicit and unspoken, and (b) they frequently antedate the relationship of person and company.

While many specific features of work were mentioned as important and regarded as matters of right — adequate pay, fair supervision, job security, and the like — many other expectations were revealed only indirectly: by the way in which people described the company or fellow-worker, by the way they behaved on the job, by the way they talked about changes that had occurred over the years.

One veteran line foreman, for example, said that he was the eldest of the seven children of a poor Arkansas farmer:

It was a pretty rough struggle, and I didn't have too much education. I got through the eighth grade. After that I helped my father on the farm. One August we had things caught up on the farm and just at that time some linemen came through. They were going to build a three-phase line 18 miles to the north. I said, "How about it, Dad?" Dad said I could go and help out so I went over one Saturday. They were cutting brush in the creek bottom. I asked the guy about a job . . . On Monday they put me right to work cutting brush, then in two or three days they put me to setting poles.

After piking poles for 17 miles they laid me off. I went back to the farm. But they came by the farm and said they wanted to have me again. That time they let me string wire as a groundman. I worked on that all fall and then went to another little town . . . I told my father I wouldn't be back until it was time to put the corn in. When I went back with the gang, I drove a truck. Then a lineman quit and I bought his tools.

He went back and forth between the company (not Midland) and the family farm several times after this. With each return to line work, he stayed longer and became more expert. Finally, he obtained a permanent job at Midland.

From this prosaic account, one might conclude that the foreman had come into electrical work quite fortuitously and primarily out of a pressing need to earn money. As this man tells his story, however, he is saying more than this. In this simple account, he is also telling us how he solved an important problem in living which confronts each person: how does one define for himself an adult occupational role?

Most people see growing up as the process of developing an occupational role which has some social status. Some indicate in various ways that they do not know how to develop such a role. Others would just as soon not grow up, preferring to remain dependent on other people as they had been on their parents.

The foreman saw himself as able to do a man's work. Though he did not have work on electric lines in mind as something which he wanted to make his trade, by going with the men and returning repeatedly to be with them he, in effect, asked them to help him establish an occupational identity. Probably he was quite unaware of this motivation.

When a man returns several times to the same work, we can assume that this action is motivated and that the underlying motivations have to do with what one seeks from life in general. Like all behavior, the choice of work reveals aspects of the personality. Attitudes toward work help to indicate how the person is attempting to resolve psychological problems which confront everyone in becoming and remaining an adult.

When a man says why he goes to work, clinical experience tells us we must listen not only to what he says. We must try also to understand what it is he cannot tell us, both because he is unaware of his unconscious motivations and because he may not feel free to tell us, who are strangers, all about his conscious reasons. From what he says as well as what he leaves unsaid, we can infer motives and expectations of whose existence and intensity he himself is not fully aware.

For example, a tabulating machine operator, when asked how he came to the company, said:

> It was more by accident than anything else. I went to the [state] employment service. They asked if I was interested in IBM or if I had any experience. I said I hadn't, but they sent me down here on Thursday . . . and I started the next Monday. I guess they were hard up for help. Usually we have eight or ten on the list [waiting for employment].

A traveling auditor said of his original job in the company:

> I got it largely by accident. I was looking for a job and I was going with a girl in ———, so I saw the vice-president up there . . . and so I got the job.

We need not concern ourselves here with the question of whether they did in fact obtain their jobs fortuitously. Our data are insufficient to answer that question. We can, however, make some inferences about motives and expectations from what they said.

Neither of these men indicated that he had a specific job in mind that represented him in some way. Neither mentioned a direction in life or an ideology out of which a direction could be developed. Neither had specific skills to offer. Neither had this company specifically in mind. Both were casting about and it may have made little difference to them whether they obtained jobs in Midland or somewhere else. There was a certain casualness about their job-seeking attitude.

One might say these men were just looking for a job. They needed to earn a living and simply took what was most available. But when a man enters an organization in this way, he says in effect, "I haven't yet decided what I am going to be in life or what I am going to do. I'll take a job here. The company can make of me what it wants." Each placed himself in the hands of the company, depending on it, as it were, to find a place in life for him and to establish his adult identity. The company in effect was expected to substitute for parental authority and to nurture them to further growth.

This relationship would probably be denied by the men if they were asked directly about it. It is likely, however, that if the company failed to act in a nurturing, stimulating way, they would become apathetic and continue to work from day to day merely for the salary, complaining that no one wanted to give them a break.

Gouldner (11) speaks of such men as *locals*, as contrasted with *cosmopolitans*. By placing themselves in the arms of the company, as it were, the company became a source of many values and their fellow employees became the reference group from which they derived much of their status. They were not committed to specific skills or to defined occupational roles which would give them a frame of reference outside the company.

Contrast the comments of men like these with those of employees who go about their job-seeking in a more methodical way. A junior acountant said:

I had come to town looking for a job. Several people from the local high school were working here in Shaw. I went to the [state] employment service and found nothing there, so I took the phone book and picked what seemed to me to be the most likely companies and went around to them one by one. I was looking for companies where a person could get ahead and Midland was one place I stopped in the process of doing that.

For this man, a job was expected to hold specific possibilities, "where a person could get ahead." He wanted something. That "something" might not have been clearly defined in his own mind, but there were at least some general ideas, and a conception of what, for him, would be success in life. Promotion, increasing income, upward social mobility — these he expected from work in this company. He had not put himself entirely in the hands of the company to make of him what it would. Instead, working for the company was seen as a means to achieve life goals which were beginning to be defined.

This man was closer to having a definite image of himself than were the men in the two preceding examples. He still required nurture and guidance but he was prepared to assume some responsibility for his success or failure, for his evolving identity.

There were implicit also in his statement a long-term relationship, for to "get ahead" would require time, and an interdependence with the organization.

Sometimes this expectation of interdependence is even more explicit when the individual begins work in the organization. A middle management man spoke both of career dissatisfactions and organizational dissatisfactions as reasons for leaving his previous job to come to Midland. He described how he started out to be an electrical engineer, but he found engineering too remote from people. He saw that in engineering he could go so far and be highly valued for it but in the situation in which he found himself he could not go into management. He wanted to move where the money was. He left engineering to enter a management activity and left his smaller company to go to Midland where he felt both a management career and greater financial rewards were possible.

This man had increasingly defined for himself both a personal image and an occupational identity. One of his motives was to acquire power over other people and control of larger organizational units. This motivation complemented an organizational need for people who could assume management responsibilities of increasing proportions. He expected specifically that the company would provide him with avenues to power. Because the range of companies to which he could go with his specialized training and experience was limited, his demands on the company for satisfaction of these needs were likely to be more intense than those of the men in the previous examples. The narrower the range of choices of companies, the greater must be his dependence on the chosen company, and the more he would have to count on fulfillment there.

This man did not place himself in the arms of the company to do with him as it wished, as did the two men described earlier. He brought to the company specific skills and experiences, together with a well defined image of himself. He sought more of a partnership with the company in which he would give something specific and receive something specific in return.

These few examples indicate some of the latent motives which underlie general expectations people have as they come to their work. Such motivations, from a clinical point of view, can be seen as attempts to deal with basic problems in living. These underlying motives are expressed as expectations of a particular kind, varying according to what a person, realistically or unrealistically, believes is possible or likely for him.

In addition to unconscious expectations having to do with the resolution of psychological problems, there are also more explicit and economic expectations. These have to do with job performance, the use of specific skills, social relations, and economic rewards. Some are characteristic of work at Midland. Some are likely to be found in any company.

Normative Expectations

A line crew, three men and a foreman, accompanied by a researcher, arrived at the location where they were to set up a new line and began preparing for the job. There was little discussion back and forth. Each man seemed to know what he was to do and what the others were doing. The foreman lent a hand when necessary while the poles were winched off the trailer and angled into place as each new hole was dug. At other times through the morning, he stood back and kept an eye on things while the most experienced lineman on the crew gave instructions to the others.

Later in the day, the foreman sat in the shade of the crew truck and talked about his job. "You've got to keep them (the men) happy," he said. "The man's got to know he's going ahead on a job, doing right. You correct mistakes without being harsh about it." He explained further that it is up to the foreman to set the pace, and that the crew expected the pace to be reasonable:

We have to be out from eight to five and we are supposed to be busy all the time. That doesn't mean you have to press people hard. They aren't being driven, but they are paid to be busy. Sometimes people have to be given a break, especially when it's hot like today and they are up on the poles, or when it's cold, but they still have a job to do.

The men on the crew were also quite definite about how a foreman should operate. One of the lineman put it this way:

A foreman should just tell you the truth and put the facts before you so you know what has to be done. I think a good foreman will let you go ahead on your own to a certain extent. He would want people to go ahead and do the work without having to tell them, "Do this, do that."

Both the foreman and the men had a clear understanding of what each had a right to expect from the other. So it was with many other work groups.

These were normative expectations — generally accepted, conscious, if usually unspoken, informal agreements arrived at out of joint experience. People could speak of them spontaneously or when questioned. They had to do with such things as what constituted a fair day's work, reasonable supervision, and appropriate responsibility.

The degree to which normative expectations are held by members of organizations of course varies according to type of industry, type of job, level of responsibility, and current industrial relations practices in the local community. These expectations will also vary according to the personal experience of organization members: new employees as compared with those who have accumulated considerable seniority, men as compared with women, those for whom work is a central life interest as compared with those whose most meaningful relationships to the environment are in other life spheres (8). We shall illustrate some of these differences as we saw them at Midland. But we want to emphasize that these expectations are likely to be encountered in other companies because of the general character of work life in our industrial culture.

Work Role Expectations

Some had chosen to work at Midland because they had skills and experiences, together with specific requirements, which they believed could best be met at Midland. A lineman who operated a service truck by himself was one of these. He said:

I was in the Marines for four years, in communications. When I came back, I wanted to go to work for the telephone company, but they wanted me to take a traveling job and that's what I had been doing in service. I wanted to stay put. The power company had an opening. I liked it because I could be located in one place and still do climbing.

Social Expectations

An employee who enters an organization immediately begins to fit into a structure of fellow workers, to be accepted or rejected by them, and ultimately, if he remains, to cast his lot with them. He cannot long survive in a work group as an outcast. He also begins to establish relationships of varying intensities with supervisors and subordinates and with others at his work level. In some organizations he will also have relationships with union business agents, shop stewards, and the union local itself.

Contentment on the job relates significantly to the quality of such relationships. Each prospective employee comes to a job expecting that he will be able to "fit in" and that he will find social gratifications as well as economic reward. A clerk, who had come to Midland after sales experience elsewhere, said:

I thought I'd rather work for a utility . . . rather than going into selling work. I think it's because of the group of people you work with, the kind of people. People you work with here are very friendly. After ten years they are a good deal of your life.

Economic Expectations

Some specifically sought at Midland economic stability which they had not been able to find elsewhere. Some had experienced the nomadic life of the electrical contracting business. Others had failed at their own businesses. This was particularly true of men who had been forced to leave their farms. For them the company offered protection and defense against a threatening environment. An oiler in a gas compressor station is an example:

Farming is so complicated any more you can't do that . . . all the big farmers have been buying up the little farms — at least that's the way it was in our part of the country. If I'd stayed in farming, I'd need to have a tin bill now and be out with the chickens.

Cultural Expectations

Economic expectations of the kind previously described shade into expectations widely held in our culture. Often people would say that they had come to Midland because they wanted "a job with a future." For most, however, this did not mean "getting ahead" in the sense of rapid promotion. This expectation had to do with job security rather than advancement.

Underlying an expressed desire for "a job with a future" is the expectation that, if the employee performs his tasks adequately and should he wish to do so, he will be able to remain in his organization until he retires. In fact, a good many employees expect that even should they be less able to do their jobs in later years, the company will carry them until retirement in return for long service.

An accountant voiced this feeling. He referred to a man whom the researchers had recently interviewed:

Look at old Joe, crippled and no good, can't work any more. The company continues to pay and feed him. The company is also very helpful and willing to work out early retirement in cases of physical disability. I can't believe that this was all done to influence present and future employees.

Midland men and women in many different work locations and at varying levels of responsibility emphasized repeatedly that they valued the job security, the noncompetitive character of operations, and the relative informality of work activities and personal relationships which they had found in the company. But these valued features of work life were regarded not as gifts or gratuities from the organization, but almost as a matter of right, received in exchange for, as one power plant operator put it, "putting in time" with the company.

Work Situation and Expectations

The position of the person or the work group in the organization and the kind of work which he did clearly influenced which kinds of expectations were given greater emphasis.

Those at higher levels in the organizational hierarchy, like people in similar positions in any organization, had wider familiarity with the range of people's organizational activities as well as responsibility for policy formulation, goal setting, and direction. They tended to identify with the major purposes of the organization as a whole as they represented it in relationships with customers, employees, governmental bodies, and financial institutions.

For example, this is how one senior executive would evaluate a subordinate: he said that he would pay a man more for keen perception than any other characteristic that that man could develop. He felt that one of the key qualities required in an executive was the ability to see ahead, to grasp an entire situation, and he felt this quality was lacking in most of those people who failed.

A foreman might have offered as his criteria for the performance of a subordinate the man's reliability and technical skill. A fellow work crew member might give primary consideration to how the man got along on the crew. The executive emphasized breadth of vision, related to decisions on behalf of the entire organization.

Long-time employees knew many other long-time employees,

now in various other parts of the company, and many officials. Many had been kept at work during the depression of the 1930's when other local businesses had laid off employees. They knew of instances when the company had given special consideration to men who were sick, injured, or no longer physically able to carry on their previous jobs. They saw such things as a matter of company policy.

These two groups, long-time employees and those at the higher levels in the company structure, as they spoke of their expectations implicitly or directly, tended to refer more to those having to do with interdependence with the organization.

A third group was characterized by some form of isolation. Some work situations were geographically distant from other parts of the company. These were settings such as gas compressor stations in which small groups of employees performed rather repetitive tasks at relatively constant rates from month to month during the year with only occasional visits from higher level supervisors. These employees lived and worked closely together. There were, in addition, some people whose work involved almost no face-to-face interaction with others.

Where the task performance required close collaborative effort, as with line crews, considerable sensitivity to the needs and moods of others was required. The very life of a crew member could depend on his being able to "size up" the feelings of a fellow crew member before starting out on a day's work. In the words of one foreman, "If a man comes to work burned off because he's had a fight with his old lady, I watch him close and I may keep him off the pole that day."

A fourth group involved primarily women. In this group, work was almost incidental to other life interests. There were young women, just out of high school, on their first job; slightly older women, recently married, who planned to stop working with the birth of their first child; and middle-aged women who had returned to work for something to do or solely to supplement family income.

People in these four work situations (those in relatively isolated settings, those who had little face-to-face interaction with others, those who worked very closely with others, and those for whom work was only an incidental interest) gave primary emphasis to expectations having to do with interpersonal relationships.

Emphasis on expectations having to do with the specific work came from those who had highly individualized work responsibilities. The job of chemist in a power plant or that of the clerk who works alone in the company office of a small community are examples. In both situations people have little continuing contact with others in the company and therefore, understandably, speak most about the job itself.

The same emphasis was true of some who had technical specialities, the performance of which could be judged by criteria established outside as well as within the organization. A specialized staff accountant, concerned with projections of various financial indices of the company's activity, or an engineer with advanced training in power plant operations or transmission line design, are examples. Such people, in Gouldner's sense, were *cosmopolitans* (11). They had an outside reference group from whom they derived certain standards and values related to their work performance.

The Company's Expectations

The company, too, has expectations which arise out of its history and business environment. These also vary in clarity and specificity. Such expectations may be viewed as company expectations, rather than those of a given management, because most would likely be held by any group of executives who were to manage the company. Circumstances would require it.

We may draw inferences about the company's expectations from the circumstances under which it must operate, from its policies and practices, its values, statements at managers' meetings and informal evaluations of someone's job performance spontaneously given to the researchers.

Midland, like other companies of its kind, operated under state laws and local franchises which set clear limits on its activities and earnings. Though privately capitalized, it was in many respects seen by its employees and customers as "not like a private company." It was, after all, a *public* utility, a stable and continuing service in the communities it served, and it had to serve everyone.

Midland's function as an essential public service required that it expect its employees to render service in emergencies. When storms or other events interrupted its service to customers, employees would have to restore that service despite personal discomfort or danger. Its function in the communities it served kept it constantly in the public eye. It would therefore expect employees to maintain standing as "good citizens" in their local communities, lest their personal conduct reflect on the reputation of the company. As a privately capitalized company, it had a responsibility to stockholders and therefore expected employees to be concerned about cost control and efficiency.

The company held a general expectation, apparent in the work history of some men, that some who entered the organization without skills or experience would acquire both sufficiently to advance to supervisory and management levels. The company, for example, paid for successfully completed correspondence courses. For some groups, linemen for example, there were formal apprentice periods. It held more specific expectations of advancement for management trainees who were given a range of training experiences and for those who had specialized training or experience which would permit them to move to higher positions. To some extent, then, the company expected to help its people shape their work lives.

Company executives mentioned in casual conversation that their experience with employees referred by friends or relatives in the company was exceptionally good. Such people, by and large, not only did their work well, but also they "fitted in" readily with other employees. They obeyed the same social norms and had the same values. Thus, the company would implicitly expect of employees that they get along well with other employees.

Because of the kinds of governmental controls under which it operated, limiting its freedom to increase its profits, Midland could not offer salary levels as high as some industries which were not so governed. Its steady growth provided opportunities for advancement, but to a lesser extent than in companies which either were expanding radically or which made frequent changes in managerial ranks. Its union contract made seniority an important consideration in promotion of those who were governed by the union contract. The company would expect its people to accept these realities.

Given its stability, the company could provide job security in return for acceptable job performance. As we have seen, there are norms for acceptable performance. In general, it expected satisfactory employees to remain with it for a long period of time. Its provisions for helping senior employees reflected this expectation. In an employee's pre-retirement years, the company frequently provided job assignments with reduced demands when advancing age made it harder for a person to continue his original assignment. Many former linemen, for example, became groundmen or worked as storekeepers when they could no longer climb. It gave special consideration to those who had catastrophic illnesses, or whose skills became obsolete with technological improvements. It expected that with increasing length of service, employees would have increasing loyalty and dedication.

The company expected of all of its people a dedication to the concept of free enterprise. The free enterprise system was frequently discussed in managers' meetings and in the employee magazine.

Of specific people, the company would have more specific expectations. These would have to do with responsibilities for specialized tasks or with anticipated advancement as a result of training and planned experiences.

This discussion of expectations is neither exhaustive nor novel. There is an extensive literature on expectations. What we emphasize here, however, is the interplay of expectations and their compelling quality. It is as if both employees and company are saying to each other, "You *must*, for I require it." When the employee goes to work, he brings expectations with him. The company tacitly accepts them when it accepts him. In turn, he tacitly accepts the company's expectations. This mutuality, with its inherent obligatory quality and its system of rewards, constitutes a psychological contract. Both parties are bound together by their mutual expectations when they enter into a relationship with each other.

The compelling aspect of the expectations arises out of their relationship to survival. The employee has to deal with the psychological fact of his being a subordinate, and sometimes a superior, as well as a colleague. He must also deal with the fact of his dependence on the company, with the changes in himself and in the world around him. Unless he does so successfully, he will have continuing difficulties fulfilling an adult social role. The company, too, must survive, and its expectations are directed to that end.

The psychological contract, furthermore, is not static. It is an evolving set of mutual expectations. When the beginning employee comes to work, he is not always certain what he wants (except that he wants a job), what he himself is offering for his side of the transaction or even what relationships he may establish with others. The new employee is not fully aware of the condition of employment, though these may be presented to him in some form of orientation. Rules and regulations sometimes have little meaning until the person can see the specific situations to which they refer. Details of policies have little significance until one sees them in application. Even plant lay-out, though described to the new employee, has little meaning at first.

As we have seen, the new employee has certain expectations, perhaps derived from the conversation of friends who are employed there, the reputation of the company in the community, and so on. Some new employees have little or no idea of the underlying psychological needs which they expect work to fulfill for them, and in some cases they have little idea of their own skills and talents. Only after they have become a part of the organization do they appreciate the intricacies of even the more obvious aspects of their relationships and the limitations of the company's ability to fulfill many of their needs. Other employees have highly defined expectations and considerable knowledge about the company's ability to fulfill them.

Management cannot know what it wants of a given person for more than a limited period of time. A man may be employed as an apprentice lineman. The company may expect him to become a lineman, but later, as he acquires experience, he will also be expected to be a teacher of other apprentices, perhaps to become a foreman or a general foreman, to fulfill other tasks and capacities as he demonstrates talents and abilities.

As Argyris' case study of a bank (1) illustrates, management may select a certain kind of people to perform a task in a staid, conservative, noncompetitive milieu. When changing economic circumstances force it to become more competitive and less conservative, management in turn holds expectations of its employees quite different from those it originally held when those same employees entered the organization.

Thus, neither party to the transaction, since the transaction is such a continuing one, fully knows what it is he wants over the length of the psychological contract, though each acts as if there were a stable frame of reference which defined the relationship.

Parenthetically, we should recognize that the psychological contract is not just a two-party arrangement between *the* person and *the* organization. As we have seen, there are also, in effect, many psychological contracts of lesser proportions between people in the organization, within work groups, and between groups and the organization. These may be viewed as collateral agreements which have a bearing on the man-organization relationship.

In summary, work experience in a company may be seen as the process of fulfilling a contractual relationship in which both parties seek continuously to meet their respective needs. From Midland people, as we indicated in chapter II, we learned that these needs seem to cluster around and be reflected in concerns about:

(a) the problem of dependency, and the balance between the necessary reliance on the environment for psychological support and structure versus the need to achieve some degree of autonomy and independence as an adult;

(b) the achievement of appropriate and psychologically rewarding relationships with other people, thus avoiding both inappropriate intimacy and chronic isolation;

(c) coping with stressful aspects of the inevitable changes which occur within oneself and in the environment with the passage of time.

These concerns are already evident in the quotations throughout this chapter. We shall elaborate upon them in succeeding chapters, noting particularly that when expectations are unrecognized, denied, or not fulfilled by the organization in this reciprocal arrangement, people act as if something which has been promised them has been withheld or denied. Such behavior, as we shall see, varies considerably from that we have defined as characteristic of healthy functioning.

CHAPTER IV

INTERDEPENDENCE

"IT does seem to me that times have changed," a manager said. "It's harder to get . . . employees to be enthusiastic now. There's more around here now interested in five o'clock coming and pay day than there used to be."

He had been reminiscing about his earlier years in the company, when Midland operations in his area had been less extensive, the number of employees smaller, and procedures had been simpler. He contrasted his memory of earlier years with some of the aspects of his current job. As he saw it, there were too many papers to read and sign, too much responsibility and not enough authority, uncooperative subordinates, top management too far away and not fully informed on local conditions. Throughout the interview, he portrayed himself as the unwilling victim of circumstance, a loyal and proven member of the organization who nevertheless was being denied support he felt he deserved from both supervisors and line people. All of this was illustrated repeatedly in his interview in such passages as this one:

In the old days, you didn't have to sign a thousand things like you do now . . . Maybe the electric department will say one day, "Here's what we have to have done today," and you go out and do that. At the same time the gas wants you to do something. I say, "O.K., but here's a stack of work orders from my boss in Shaw that say I have to do that, too . . ." [meanwhile] the men say, "I won't worry about that, I'll leave it to the managers."

It was hard for this manager to make decisions — even about the study. When the researchers sat down in his office to plan a schedule of interviews with company people in the area, it seemed to be very difficult to get the details settled. He had little flexibility in this, for him, stress situation. The manager seemed unable to understand just what it was the researchers wanted to do and seemed to be concerned with the possibility that perhaps after all they were in the division to evaluate operations and report back to top management at Shaw.

Subordinates reacted to the manager's behavior in a variety of ways. Some overidentified themselves with him, putting themselves in his harassed position without seeing some of the ways in which he himself contributed to his harassment. These were the people who felt sorry for the manager and felt they had no right to make demands upon him. Said one, "I try to stay away from the manager because that man is so busy he can't breathe."

Some reacted with anger, alleging that they could get no attention from him. A member of a field crew remarked:

This is the first place in my life I have worked that your supervisor or manager doesn't come down and talk to a guy. I've worked on different jobs. They will either come along and give you a boot or a pat on the back. Personally, I'd rather have them come down and give me a good chewing than not come down at all.

Some quarreled with each other because inadequate supervision left their responsibilities poorly defined. These quarrels led to loss of much of the gratification that people could have found in working with each other. Two subordinates who worked closely together hardly spoke to each other, each blaming the other for not doing what he was supposed to do, and asserting that what was not being done was the job of the other. Spontaneous productivity was inhibited.

In an effort to keep in touch with what was going on, since he could not bring himself to do so personally, the manager called for more reports. One foreman pointed out a production record he had to keep, and then drew out a secret record he kept in addition to the official one. The official record met the manager's daily expectations, the unofficial one recorded what actually had been done. Some days the production was more than the official expectation; some days it was less. In the end, the goals were met, but the daily variations could not be openly recorded.

Many were unable to recognize the contribution they could make to the organization. Their feelings about being rejected limited their ability to see their assets. Some of these feelings were summed up by one crewman who concluded:

I think the trouble is that they don't come around and try to understand our plight. Maybe they don't want to. There always has to be a fall guy. Maybe we're it. I don't know.

The problems resulting from the inability to depend on the manager spread throughout the unit. There was frequent mention of jobs started but unfinished as crews rushed from one job to another. There was a "forced draft" productivity at the expense of the men's natural desire to complete one job before going on to the next. Foremen complained that the men were not following safety precautions as well as they could, and from both the men and the foreman came reports of friction, tension, hostility, and unpleasantness. Thus, not only did the men lose much of the possible gratifications in their work, but they were unable to treat others as individuals. The men themselves reported their hostility as they talked of flouting authority, feeling oppressed when told to do something, and being annoyed by many minor events which in other circumstances might have been passed over.

The relationship between the manager's behavior and the difficulties they were having with their men was not readily apparent to any of the middle management men in this situation who could not understand the hostility of the men. The manager himself had said, "It's harder to get the . . . employees to be enthusiastic now," attributing their lack of motivation to forces outside the work situation. Nor could the foremen, by their own efforts, either hide or compensate for managerial weakness, for they, too, were in conflict and their men reacted to their inability to be dependable authority figures when they themselves had no such figure.

One veteran supervisor of field crews wound up his interview this way:

> To get on the right side of the men I've broken my neck. I've tried every kind of psychology you want to see. There's more to this than some of us old bastards can understand.

In his search for some answer to his dilemma, this man was hoping the research would point to a better way of doing things. The researchers, in his eyes, became the source of authority, wisdom, and support he had been seeking:

> I'd appreciate it if you boys would come out with some suggestions about what we could do on this. I think you can come up with something on these interviews. Tell us where we can make some improvements, where we made our mistakes. I hope you fellows come up with some decisions about this. It will mean a lot to us.

For this member of the local unit as for some others, the lack of structure and chronic conflict within and between work groups were powerful inducements to seek some clearer definition of the situation from anyone who might have expert or authoritative advice to give. The search for something to depend on was so overwhelming that many people forgot what they had been told earlier in the orientation meetings, that the team would not give advice to the company (see appendix II). They looked to the researchers "to come up with some decisions."

In this section of the company, people seemed unable to depend on the structure of the organization or leadership for guidance and controls. Some who tried to create structure for themselves incurred the resentment of their fellow workers who saw them as "taking over."

Those who identified themselves with the harassed but "very nice" manager were unhappy with the administrative turmoil and the fact that they could not depend on management to maintain consistent policies and communication. Though withdrawing to their own niches to operate as best they could, they were angry toward the manager and felt guilty because of their hostile feelings.

To attempt to create structure was to flout or undermine authority, as well as to create resentment. To withdraw was to live with angry feelings and guilt.

It should be noted that, despite those problems, the people in this company area were able to render the needed services to customers and, according to the balance sheets, to operate profitably. There were many reasons why the manager in this case could not do other than he did. This illustrates, however, the results of such actions regardless of the reason for them.

The Problems of Dependency

Both McGregor (23) and Argyris (2) have discussed problems of dependency in industrial organizations. The latter has summarized a wide range of studies. Argyris has argued that business organizations by their very nature foster dependency. Such critics consider any form of dependency detrimental to the "self actualization" of the person, or his ability to become fully what he is capable of becoming. These criticisms fail to recognize that dependence on others is constant, universal, and necessary in some degree for personal growth. It is found in all spheres of human activity.

The human being is not born with the necessary psychological and physiological equipment for early independent existence. During a large and significant part of life the human being is markedly dependent on others. It is universally recognized that the child requires adults to meet his basic biological needs. It is less widely recognized how dependent he is on adults to meet imperative psychological needs. Particularly important in his survival is *psychological* nourishment, without which an infant can die (33). It is not surprising, therefore, to find that having other human beings to gratify crucial emotional needs has always been important in any activity, whatever the setting and the circumstances. Nor should it be surprising that people should seek to gratify their dependent needs in the organization where they work as they do in their families and among their friends.

While each person moves toward greater independence as he grows, and the mature person is supposed to be able to "stand on his own feet," as a matter of clinical fact no person is ever completely independent and each must come to terms with his dependent needs. A person's choice of work is often a way of dealing with this universal psychological problem. Some people for various psychological reasons must deny that they have any such needs. They might choose to be independent entrepreneurs. Others, more comfortable depending on an organized structure, will take their places in highly organized, stable organizations or in close dependent relationships with bosses in small organizations.

The resolution of the conflict between dependent needs and the social requirement that one be independent is not easy. The conflict, usually unconscious, is evident in all psychiatric treatment and it is pervasive in human society. Little wonder then that dependence — interdependence — autonomy should be one of the central concerns of Midland people, and even less wonder that when dependent needs fail to be met turmoil results.

To grow up is to become interdependent rather than completely independent. Being an adult means to give and take. A person can feel that it is appropriate to gratify his dependency needs in an organization if the organization, in turn, is in some way dependent on him. As one of the men said, "There's a lot of things they could tell us that would help us. A lot of things we could tell that would help them." Without such an exchange, the person cannot feel that he is an adult and becomes resentful for being treated, as he sees it, like a child.

People vary widely in the degree to which dependency needs manifest themselves and the particular forms these manifestations take. Some people go to the extreme of leaning heavily on others for a lifetime, in a very obvious fashion. Others deny dependency needs, as if to recognize the existence of them is in itself immature. Between the two extremes is recognition and acceptance of legitimate dependency needs and gratification of them in socially acceptable ways — carrying one's own responsibilities in life, but turning to others when others can be helpful and help is needed.

Legitimacy

Some things done at Midland to meet people's dependency needs were mutually acceptable to both people and the organization. These acceptable actions constituted a social norm. Probably there is also such a norm in every organization, although it may vary widely from business to business. Some aspects of Midland's personnel policies formally recognized that dependency expectations were a part of the psychological contract. This awareness was most conspicuous in security provisions such as health and accident benefits, retirement plans and the like, jointly agreed upon in negotiation. The recognition became more personalized when the company came to the support of a sick employee or made it possible for an aging one to have an easier job.

The employees regarded it as legitimate and socially acceptable to overcome or compensate for certain deprivations related to dependency (the depression of the 1930's, loss of marginal farms in the 1950's) by joining Midland. A person could join Midland if he were seeking economic security, anticipating that he would be in an organization whose fortunes did not fluctuate sharply with each minor change in the economic cycle; he could find some relief from constant arduous labor in a company where the work pace would vary from the intensity of an emergency to comparatively relaxed routine chores. He could avoid the "do or die" aspects of competition in a situation where competition was directed more to vanquishing the elements, evolving more efficient practices and better service than to individual achievement (as contrasted with factory piece work, for example). He could ameliorate feelings of helplessness and loneliness in a company where supervision over the years had grown more permissive, and in which fellow workers shared many of his own needs and views. That, too, was part of the psychological contract.

Given these norms, there were at least two extremes or deviant types of behavior which defined legitimate dependencies and gave rise to disturbance and conflict. They were seen psychologically as *denial* and *exploitation*.

Denial

One sees in clinical experience that for some people to want to be dependent in any way is to feel inferior, second best, infantile, or effeminate. They experience such sharp internal condemnation of their unconscious, almost overwhelming dependency wishes that they cannot express these needs. With such people, no external object or agent can in fact supply that which they so ardently desire. Their demands, if they could be expressed, would exceed the capacity of any person or organization to meet them under ordinary circumstances. If the need to deny his dependent needs is so strong that a person cannot accept the supports and gratifications of dependency needs offered in a business like Midland, among other alternatives, he might well seek out a company which provides little or no supports, for example, one in which he may depend entirely on commissions for income. If, however, denial of these needs is not so strong as to require the person to seek such a solution, he might remain in a stable, structured company, taking the available supports and gratifications for granted.

If he remains in the organization, such a person will likely accept responsibility and carry out his tasks well. In his own eyes he will see himself as independent. He will have difficulty accepting guidance and direction from superiors because he will interpret decisions which go against his judgment and criticism of his work or actions as threats to his independence. Unable to accept his dependency needs, he will find it difficult to depend upon subordinates. Viewing himself as one who stands on his own two feet, he will expect his subordinates to do as well. At the same time, he will be unable to permit them to be really independent in their

decisions and actions for to fortify his own self-image he must
carry all the responsibility himself.

The manager in the example at the beginning of the chapter is
a case in point. When pressures on him increased, he dealt with
his anxiety by increased activity and increasing assumption of
responsibilities that rightfully belonged to others. His inability to
accept his incompletely met dependent needs was reflected in his
inflexibility, his need to control and his hyperactivity. His deep
underlying insecurity spread to create unrest and uncertainty.

Exploitation

At the other extreme is the person whose very pressing dependency needs, also insatiable, are expressed to everyone. For this
person there is no thought of independence of the organization.
In fact, in his view the organization is in constant debt to him. He
is constantly exploiting his environment. He is never satisfied
with the organization and the people in it who do not (who can
not) give him as much nurture and support as he craves. Though
demanding and exploiting, he can give nothing in return for he
needs so much himself. It is this individual who has developed
ways of rationalizing his behavior to appease his conscience and
evade his obligations. He is constantly demanding promotion and
increased salary while at the same time he resents any demands
which go with promotion or more salary. His psychological security, despite his protests, lies in the structure of the organization
which requires of him at least minimal performance and quite
rigidly prescribes his occupational behavior. Such a person vio-
lently attacks bureaucracy but cannot function without it.

To take one of many examples, an office clerk describes how
such people create difficulties for those around them at work:

> We have had a few who didn't fit around here. Maybe they didn't
> carry their share of the load or they weren't the kind of people you
> like to have, who say they will do a job and then come back later and
> say it's finished [when they have not done it]. I don't know why they
> were that way. Maybe they have been in some other kind of a job

where they didn't need to do anything. They more or less expect things to come to them I think.

To deny dependent needs or to exploit others for gratification of dependent needs (as contrasted with interdependence) were both illegitimate by the standards of Midland people. Our experience in other companies indicates that denial and exploitation are similarly regarded by most employees. Both modes of behavior make it impossible to treat others as individuals.

Toward Interdependence

If dependent needs are universal, if part of becoming an adult is to find appropriate interdependent relationships, and if there are normative, legitimate expressions of such needs in business organizations, how can a person capitalize on these circumstances to move toward greater independence?

We have seen that formal aspects of the organization become a base on which the individual may depend. The formal structure permits each person to know his area of operation and those to whom he may turn for direction. Organizational policies guarantee certain security provisions. Informal aspects of the organization such as relationships to co-workers make for interdependence both on and off the job.

These features of organizational life, however, are not sufficient by themselves either to gratify legitimate dependent needs or to foster movement toward independence. In the example at the beginning of the chapter, the formal structure remained clear and the security provisions were the same as for the rest of the company. Many people had worked together in that unit for years. Leadership which denied dependent needs vitiated much of the gratification which might have come from the structure, the policies, or other people. A pivotal point then is the authority figure in the work setting and his relationship to his subordinates.

Parenthetically, it should be obvious that although the attitude of the authority figure is crucial in maintaining interdependence, sometimes company policies may deny him the possibility of gratifying dependent needs. If, for example, he could not supply his men with adequate tools to do their job or if he could not give reliable answers to the men's questions, in either case because of company policies, then no matter how much he accepted dependent needs, he could do little about some of them.

We may contrast with this example other kinds of relationships between subordinates and supervisors discussed by Midland people. In these contrasting patterns of authority, differences appear in how the problem of dependence is expressed and dealt with.

Several long-term employees described their boss this way:

He could chew you out as mean as you please and the next minute everything would be all the same. It would blow right over. He seemed to know all parts of the business . . . He had worked up as an office boy and worked in all parts of the business. He knew how to manage people . . . He could look at a report and pick out a mistake right away. I never understood how he could do that . . . He used to be down here before 8 a.m. every morning . . . I know he depended on me because one time he wouldn't leave on vacation unless I was there to take over.

He wanted his instructions to be followed, right or wrong, and if it was the wrong decision, it was his decision, not yours . . . I worked for him thirty years. We had our arguments. Sometimes I would get over a point but he wouldn't say, "Okay, I'll go along with you." He'd say, "Okay, hard head, have it your way." There's no way to compare him with other people.

He didn't hesitate to chew you out once in awhile, but if he told you something you could write that down as something like a law.

He told me, "You're just like the milk man. You go to a certain place on a certain day, the boys know you are coming." I said, "That's right, but the thing runs okay, doesn't it?" He said, "That's the hell of it, I haven't got anything more to say to you about it."

The boss knew his job, performed it, and demanded that his subordinates perform their jobs. They could depend on him and his knowledge, but they were aware that he, too, depended on them. He did not blame them for his errors; they knew he was consistently fair. He was able to accept some differences of opinion and some hostility from his subordinates, demonstrating at the same time that he had affection for them. He insisted that his subordinates visit with *their* subordinates, even if there were no problems to be dealt with.

Implicit in this illustration are four of the aspects of behavior in our criteria. Flexibility under stress alone was not mentioned.

We infer from the fondness with which these subordinates remember their old boss that they identify themselves with him, at least in part. The warmth with which they remember these aspects of his leadership suggests that they would like to be able to emulate these characteristics. Such identification, in clinical experience, is a psychological commonplace. People will usually seek to identify themselves with figures in authority much as they sought to identify themselves with parents, teachers, scout leaders, and older friends. In identifying himself with the adult, the child comes to assume adult modes of behavior and becomes increasingly adult and independent himself. When it is possible to identify with a superior in the business organization, the subordinate models himself in part on the superior. By making a part of himself the superior's broader experience, knowledge, skills, and behavior, the subordinate broadens his own perspective and increases his own abilities, thereby moving toward increasing independence.

The superior cannot become a model, however, if he cannot meet the dependent needs of his subordinates. If he denies *his own* dependency needs, as did the manager described at the beginning of the chapter, the subordinates become more dependent. They are afraid to take any initiative and wait for someone else to take the responsibility. They become inwardly angry and passively resist any effort to motivate them. As one of the veteran supervisors had said, "I've tried every kind of psychology you want to see. There's more to this than some of us old bastards can understand."

If the authority figure is aggressive in his denial of subordinates' dependency needs, he is perceived as a bad, depriving figure, yet strong and very powerful. He produces increased dependence, fear, a sense of loss, anger, guilt, and self punishment (sometimes in the form of accidents) in others, as in this example in which a middle management man talks about his predecessor:

He loved to yell at people and he did not like to delegate authority. His immediate subordinate had been in that job seven years and in all that time he had not been allowed to make any decisions. If he did they were countermanded immediately. The boss would go out in the field and see something that didn't quite suit him and the boys would say, "———— told us to do it that way," and he would say, "Don't pay any attention to that s.o.b., he won't be here long."

[After I came] if someone had his feelings hurt, they wouldn't go to their foreman . . . the first couple of months here they wore my chair out coming up here . . . When I came here I vowed that for at least a year I wouldn't raise my voice and I haven't yet. He was always beating people over the back to hurry, hurry, hurry. That had some direct effect. We had an accident with that hurry.

The key role of the authority figure in determining the way in which the problem of dependency is handled was shown in one power plant. Here, we saw the different ways in which the supervisor was perceived by the people below him. Particularly striking were the varying degrees of dependency required by subordinates. Let us begin with his own description of his job:

My job is to get the job done and satisfy the help, that's the main thing . . . I have to get these boys all experienced, teach them. Now they know as much about the plant as I do. They tell me things lots of times. The way I see it, ten heads are better than one. They can go and continue with the work whether I am here or not. If you don't have it that way you have a helluva headache . . . if there is any trouble, it is due to the supervisor. It would come from not being around the boys and joking [with them] . . . we've got to be broad-minded. If you make a mountain out of a mole-hill out of everything that comes along you're going to be in a turmoil.

This man's subordinates were divided on how he should operate. From one employee we heard:

I heard someone say once that to be a good supervisor, you have to be a good son-of-a-bitch. That's not true. I don't believe the supervisor should mix with the men. He should be friendly, firm if he has to be. Maybe there is a time when he has to be a nice s.o.b., but chances are he has to be that way for a good reason. You've got to be able to talk over differences with the men — listen to other ideas. Then if he has to be firm — he has to be firm . . . he has got to treat everybody fair and square.

Another employee had a different story:

. . . I tell you frankly that I would feel that it's [a good relationship with the company] being held down by [the supervisor]. He should get his boys to believe in him and really think he is the supervisor and get them to admire him like an officer in the service. He shouldn't give them the idea that he is just somebody else there. But to get their respect he's got to do it in watching who he runs around with [on the job] and in civilian life — I mean private life. But he's not straightforward, I don't see how the men can appreciate him as a supervisor.

These examples illustrate the conflicting and intense demands upon any supervisor, and the need of the men for an identification figure. As we shall see more clearly in the next chapter, employees seek from their superiors, on both the unconscious and conscious levels, basic affection and respect. If the superior provides minimum controls of what they do, some employees will malign the supervisor for not giving them the leadership they require to satisfy their dependency needs. If, on the other hand, he checks everything which they do and insists upon solving their problems in a specific way, he will be attacked by some with equal vigor for making them overdependent. But there is a middle ground. Under some conditions, *interdependence* is possible.

Dependency and Hostility

When both the organization and its people recognize dependency needs and appropriate efforts are made to gratify those aspects of dependency which are legitimate, an associated problem must be considered. Even the best of situations is not free of conflict and hostility.

When things are going well, when both employees and company accept their dependence on each other, people are reluctant to express openly whatever feelings of hostility may arise toward important figures in authority. Consequently, there is a tendency for subordinates to contain whatever anger may be aroused in them and to direct it inwardly or to displace it onto the work in the form of mistakes, absenteeism, lethargy, *et cetera*. These are forms of withdrawing from a work situation which has become painful — withdrawal implies a loss of gratification. Thus, there is need for channels through which hostility may be expressed without guilt or the fear of retaliation.

Such channels may be regular joint discussions among employees and various levels of management, procedures for adjudicating grievances, or systems of communicating complaints which assure they will be properly heard by responsible authorities. A labor union often serves such a function. If, for some reason, these channels cannot or do not serve this function, then the feelings of angry frustration on the part of the employees may become exacerbated.

One of the meter repairmen in the Gramercy division very neatly summarized such a situation:

A man lost an arm in an auto accident. The company terminated him. He was a damned good man. We really appreciated him because he wasn't afraid of work. That made the men feel bitter. It will be years before they get that out of their system. [The union had failed to respond to their complaints because the accident had not occurred on the job.] We had several conferences to get the man's job back and he's been working for the past two years as an engineer's helper . . . If we could have transferred that fellow, it would have been a lot better feeling.

The event remained vivid two years after its occurrence, illustrating how threatening it must have been to the men to feel that their investment in security might well not pay off. Not only did the men begin to think they had been deserted by the protective authority, the company, but also they were unable to use the union as an effective channel for making their feelings known. Another man explained:

The union people are bitter both at the company and the union leaders. They felt the union leadership and Shaw should have gotten together and settled that situation about the boy who lost his arm. They are bitter at the union and I think they are justified.

A welder pointed out that it was difficult to express feelings even in the union meetings: he said he was not against the union because you have to have someone to bargain for you and,

> I can't go in and see Mr. Kane and say, "Mr. Kane I need a raise . . ." I would like to see the men all come to the meetings but they would have to make the meetings more interesting . . . Most of the fellows are a little bit speech shy and don't want to get up and talk. The only way to do that is to make an itemized list and get up and say them. I don't think anyone wants to go on strike or anything like that. That's drastic.

The recurrent nonaggression theme indicated that the men did not want to be and could not be grossly and openly hostile to superiors whom they liked and on whom they depended, but they did want some protected way of expressing their hostilities and seeking redress. They could not stand up to shout and protest openly.

Another repairman recognized that the company had no formal responsibility for the injured man:

> Sure he was out riding around on his own time when it happened . . . It may have been inevitable with just one arm they could not hire this man, but it seems to me this is no way to do things . . . usually they take pretty good care of their injured employees. That is why I cannot understand how, in the case of the man that lost his arm, they acted in such a way.

The company had a side in this case, as was recognized by this employee, but it is not our purpose here to argue the merits of the issue and assign blame to the men, the company, or the union. Rather, we use this example to illustrate how hostility can be generated when dependency needs, which have become part of the psychological contract, are not met and when a channel for displacing and communicating hostile feelings does not function.

As the repairman noted, there was a feeling among the men that there had always been a place for people who were injured or handicapped in some way. They need not worry about what was going to happen to them. According to their concept of the psychological contract, the company would protect them. This was part of legitimate dependency. When the norm was no longer held to, it became difficult to predict what authority would do. When the union failed to function as a channel for the solution of the problem, feelings of frustration increased. The result was behavior which was passively resistant (less spontaneously productive), resentful (loss of some gratifications), irritable (impairment of flexibility).

INTERDEPENDENCE AND GROWTH

Interdependence with the organization, as we have seen from these examples, is an important emotional anchor point for the people who work there. With adequate formal security provisions, the person is relatively free of concern with economic security. With adequate organizational structure, he is relatively free of concern about what his job is and where his responsibilities lie. The fulfillment of the psychological contract, however, requires more than organizational formalities. Interdependence with the organization requires and implies relationships with people. The interpretation of the contract is the function of people in authority who act on behalf of the organization. It is they who give life to the words of the formal contract and meaning to the organizational structure. They mediate the dependence of the people on the company and vice versa. They are the agents of interdependence.

When authority figures accept the fact that they have dependent needs as do subordinates, and when that acceptance is not defeated in some fashion by company policies, they permit both the formal contract and the organizational structure to serve their respective functions. In view of security provisions, a person need not devote a large part of his energy to worry about the future.

Given well defined organizational structure, he does not need to dissipate his energy in the defensive maneuvers of withdrawal and passive resistance, or in expressions of aggression in the form of irritability, flouting authority, accidents, and outbursts of anger. Much of the energy thus freed from conflict may then be directed to the joint responsibilities of the individual employees and the company. More than that, the individual is able to direct some of his energy to modeling himself after the good superior, and by so doing, to his own continued growth.

Certainly appropriate gratification of legitimate dependency needs increases the range of sources of pleasures, and interdependence requires that other people be treated in terms of their needs. Interdependence, implying support from others and the organization, also makes it possible to deal with stress more easily, and energies freed from conflict may be devoted to personal productivity. But interdependence is most clearly related to the realistic recognition of assets and limitations, and thereby to growth.

With interdependence, a person can extend himself, as it were. For some, such extension may be in the direction of increased responsibility for larger segments of the organization. For others, it may be in the direction of greater pleasure in their work, fuller use of capacities or increased self-esteem, all of which contribute not only to the achievement of a worthy occupational identity but also to mental health.

CHAPTER V

DISTANCE

In one of the Midland division offices, fifteen women worked together in a large area containing desks, tables, and office equipment. Most of the women could see each other as they worked. The work area was also in plain view of customers and the street outside but yet was insulated from direct contact with outsiders because of the cashiers' desks which separated the working area from the customers' area. Group members performed three different kinds of tasks. Some had customer contact as a major part of their job (cashiers, switchboard operator). Others were doing clerical jobs involving little or no customer contact (billing clerk, payroll clerk). The duties of a few were primarily staff or administrative (senior clerk, secretaries to the division manager, division superintendent, and division auditor).

Almost all of the women were attractively — and in some cases rather ostentatiously — dressed: carefully ironed cotton dresses or skirt and blouse combinations in gay colors; fancy sandals or high-heeled pumps, earrings; well groomed hair and skin. Men were apparently excluded from the group's immediate work area. The auditor, whose office was adjacent to the area occupied by the women, dealt with the women for the most part through the senior clerk, who was their immediate supervisor. The manager and the division engineer had offices on the same floor but rarely dealt directly with the women.

Life at work was made up of small events, which were described with warmth and pleasure, indicating their significance. Some of the women came to work early and spent their time chatting and lounging until the day's work began. If the day's task involved some increased work load the pressure was offset by the knowledge that it was only temporary, for there would be periods during which there was little to do. The accomplishment of the day's tasks terminated the cycle begun in the morning. The tasks were performed under the guidance and control of the senior clerk and the auditor, both of whom were readily available to state precisely what had to be done and how it was to be done, so that each woman had minimum responsibility for decisions. Another daily event was the coffee break, spiced with chatting and gossiping.

The daily routine included contacts with people outside the group: other company employees, customers, buyers of appliances, friends and neighbors who passed by, and even those who called on the telephone. If one were troubled or overloaded with work, one of the other girls was always there to help, either to listen or to lend a hand.

The intraoffice events were so emotionally significant to the women that the group was quite oblivious of the major events elsewhere in the company (for example, changes in top management) and even outside of it which might have some effect upon them. While they knew of these events, they did not have any significant feeling or conflict about them.

There was a degree of play and freedom of expression — the pretty dresses and the laughter, opportunity to learn about one's self and others, the resource of advice and help in periods of tension. These seemed to be much like the events of adolescence in the context of another form of a "good home," the company. Yet the work was done with interest and enthusiasm, and each recognized that their joint central responsibility was the work.

Almost all of the women mentioned the work group in one way or another. Six of them were active participants in group social life. They comprised a social in-group. Six more either explicitly rejected many of the social values and activities of the in-group or spoke entirely of other things in connection with their work. These were women who worked primarily for money or had social interests elsewhere in the community. Finally, a marginal sub-group of three women engaged in some of the informal socializing, but did not fully share the social values of the in-group.

The Job as a Social Situation

Those who comprised the in-group described its function for them. An accounting clerk said:

There are some firm friendships here. You get to eat together, go to parties and have fun. This is a good way to make friends and what I like about all this is that this does not make any trouble with the company . . . it's just wonderful because people like me and I like them.

The secretary to the division manager commented:

It's a wonderful group of girls.

She went on to speak of wiener roasts after work, of being welcomed back after a vacation trip, and all of the parties for various events related to the job.

Another clerk said, "It's a grand group of girls." She spoke about the freedom and informality of the job. Then she drew an unusual comparison between Midland and other companies. As she saw it, she attributed the freedom and informality to the "public nature" of the organization.

A private concern expects more reserve. Here, if you want to laugh you can laugh.

The senior clerk added another dimension to the in-group:

Some of my best girl friends I met working at Midland.

The members of the in-group were women whose lives away from the job were relatively barren. A key member of the group, for example, was a widow without children who had lost several members of her family and who spoke directly of the meaning of work to her in her time of trouble. Her closest friend in the group had few girl friends other than those on the job and had predominantly solitary, masculine interests away from the job. A third single woman spoke very little of family or home.

Part of the setting for this group which made such socializing possible was the fact that the women came from a common socioeconomic background and many had common pre-job experience. Many of them had held a job or two before coming to Midland. Many had gone to school together and knew each other in the community before coming to the job. Working conditions and salary for the office women were better than they could obtain other places in the community. As a result the group had an "elite" status in their own eyes and perhaps in the eyes of others.

The jobs themselves were circumscribed. Women had no power in the company. Beyond the position of senior clerk, there were no advancement possibilities. There were specific office jobs, clearly "feminine," which could be held only by women.

These factors taken together enhanced the social aspects of the job. The group structure was further reinforced by the way in which the group handled its relationship with higher management. The informal solidarity of the group was an insulator against outside influences, particularly from authority figures. There was in effect group management over relationships with authority figures, particularly male supervisors, such as the division manager and the division auditor. By virtue of these group needs, as well as their formal roles, certain members of the group were allocated the function of dealing with these figures. They required it without prejudicing their position in the eyes of the other women.

The manager's secretary said that she found herself in a peculiar position because of her job. People came to her about matters they did not want to bring to the manager but that they would like him to find out about. She gave as an example a special Good Friday service which was held every year. Many of the merchants closed from 1 to 3 p.m. so employees could go to the service. When the question of closing the office came up the women in the office said, "Will you ask Mr. ———?"

The in-group felt that new people in the office should recognize the existence of the group spirit and that there should be group recognition of the new people after a suitable interval. One way in which they recognized new people was to ask them to some off-the-job parties. But some of the employees did not want to attend these parties and as a result remained on the periphery of the group. This ritual of acceptance involved everyone, including supervisors.

A new manager did not at first understand the solidarity of the women or the way in which they managed their work relationships. For a while he created havoc, bypassing the auditor and going directly to the women for information. After he had settled down in his new job, the girls sent word by the manager's secretary that they wanted to see the manager. In her words,

Mr. ——— jumped up and put the union contract booklet in his pocket and went out of the office. He looked around and said, "Where do you want to meet?" The senior clerk said, "I think we ought to meet in the [demonstration] kitchen." They went around there and all of the girls were standing there and they had made coffee and there was a big cake saying "Happy Birthday, Mr. ———." He was absolutely floored. In fact, he even pulled out the little booklet and said, "I thought you wanted me to come out here on some kind of grievance."

A Contrast

Another group of women worked in a comparable office in a community of similar size and similar socioeconomic circumstances. Their work was the same as that of the first group, and their environment equally feminine.

In the interviews, several of the women mentioned that members of the group formerly had been very close to each other, participating together in many off-time activities. In recent months there had been no more of such socializing. The women told their own story. A secretary discussed difficulties which had arisen with the arrival of a new supervisor and then commented:

All we're working for now is the salary. It used to be we enjoyed ourselves at work, but maybe that isn't so true any more . . . We used to have more parties and things than we do now. Many is the time when everybody would just come over to my house. Just a bunch of silly gals and we'd sit around and have a high old time. We put on our jeans and had wiener roasts and things like that. We don't do that as much as we used to. I don't know why.

This woman was beginning to sense the relationship between the group's feelings about the supervisor and the decay of social cohesion, but the two ideas were not yet clearly related in her own mind for she still could say, "I don't know why." A payroll clerk made a similar statement:

The new boss doesn't understand personnel problems . . . He talks everything over with one girl and she spreads the word around. One other girl took a very personal matter to him and then this other girl spread it around . . . Actually I think few friendships occur over the nonoffice hours. The girls who have been here several years say they have never seen anything like it before and the office is in a constant uproar. Before, they had picnics and things like that but they have none of that now.

The anger of the women about the supervisor was voiced by one of the clerks:

To be frank with you, our boss a lot of times leaves a bad feeling. Before, our bosses have always been pleasant but, well, he's not sometimes . . . when he's in a bad mood it affects us all.

After describing how much difficulty she had getting a decision from the boss, she said that the women went on coffee breaks according to a schedule set up by him without consulting the women about whom they would like to have coffee with.

A cashier added another observation:

One trouble is that the supervisor here is very partial to one girl. There are a lot of times we get real busy. One time we were real busy and she got a leave of absence and we had to take some of her work. I think that a supervisor should be more impersonal, don't you? . . . it makes a lot of difference when the local manager comes in and speaks to you in the morning or if he doesn't speak to you at all. The engineer is very nice, too. He's friendly but he's impersonal and I like that. The former engineer was too friendly. I guess maybe girls notice things like that more than a man does. With a man like that you can't speak to him without him thinking that you're saying, "Come on." So I like the way the engineer works with people.

Balanced Distance

Some of the women in the first group spontaneously mentioned their social activities as an important aspect of the job. They had made friendships, took meals together, had parties. And all of this "didn't make any trouble with the company." There was frequent spontaneous mention of "a wonderful group of girls," and having found "best friends" in the office. For those whose lives seemed less emotionally rich than others, the personal associations at work apparently provided a valued emotional experience. Those who did not wish to participate as fully in the socializing did not need to, and could remain more peripheral to the group. Each was relatively free to pick and choose from the multiple sources of gratification.

Furthermore, the women exercised informal group control over their own activities, even to the point of "initiating" and accepting the manager. This control was not rigid. Those who wanted to share in some of the social activities some of the time could do so, and withdraw from others. Those who wanted no real part in socializing were not forced in any way to do so. The women demonstrated a sensitivity to individual differences in their treatment of each other.

The important consideration for this group was the way in which people could of their own accord govern their own relationships with others. They could choose how close they wanted to get to those with whom they worked, or how far away from others they wanted to remain. That is, they could maintain a balanced psychological distance from others, one which was comfortable for each of them.

In their concern with establishing and maintaining relationships with others on the job, Midland employees spoke frequently about the problem which we conceptualize here as "balanced psychological distance." There is some balance, some optimal distance, which is comfortable, satisfying and workable for each person in any particular situation. Each person has the fundamental problem of balancing constructive and destructive forces in the personality, love and anger, and one important way is controlling how close or far away one is from other people. As we have seen in the case of the first group of women, people differ in their needs for relative closeness or distance.

Some are relatively comfortable and gain immeasurably with considerable emotional interchange with others, while others prefer relatively cool, distant interactions. The latter tend to find gratification in their work not so much from their involvement in interpersonal relationships as from such things as mastering the equipment with which they work, or the technical details of the job.

Similarly, some enjoy sharing relatively personal and intimate aspects of their lives, aspects which to others represent too much psychological exposure. The same information about his personal life is casually dropped in conversation by one person, while it is felt to be extremely close and private to another. In the extreme, we can consider *isolates* and *socializers*.

When the distance was comfortable for those who sought socializing relationships, the others could more readily establish whatever was a balanced distance for them. When the socializers could not maintain a cohesive group, the isolates, too, found it difficult to establish an appropriate distance.

The reader might well ask at this point what difference such a concern on the part of employees makes. Are they not being employed to do a job, and isn't everything else secondary? Should they not be held strictly to the work at hand and socializing be minimized? If anyone has a concern about his distance from others, should he not keep that out of the business and worry about it "after 5"?

In his relationship to his company, the employee inevitably must deal with other people, and, as we have indicated in chapter III, he comes to an organization with expectations that he will be able to find comfortable relationships with others. He cannot shed his psychological expectations when he enters the door each morning. Rather, because of the major psychological importance to him of the organization in which one works, he must perforce seek gratifying relationships in it.

The experience of the second group of women makes this clear. ". . . all we're working for now is the salary," a secretary said, pointing out that there used to be more comfortable relationships, something more than money to work for, and these were now gone. The clerk said, "The girls who have been here several years say they have never seen anything like it before and *the office is in a constant uproar.*" They could no longer accomplish their work with the same spontaneous initiative which had characterized it before.

The focus on the *job*, the basic reason for which the women were together, was lost when psychological distance became imbalanced. The preoccupation with the imbalance was at the expense of the work. The keystone of balanced distance lies in the focus on the job. That is the reality which is everyone's guide — the task to be done. Putting concern with personal relationships ahead of the common task is destructive to both people and the organization.

In various ways, the women in the second group kept saying that the psychological distance between them had grown too great. Its effects were felt not only on the job, but off the job as well. They did not have parties or informal evenings with each other as they had had. The relationship between the auditor and his secretary was too close and appropriate distance was no longer maintained, and the rest of the women felt betrayed. He became too distant from them. In addition, his arbitrary assignment of coffee breaks and his violation of the confidence of one woman was an attack on the group. They apparently felt they could do little about their anger toward him, but they could protect themselves by withdrawing from each other.

Their withdrawal from each other was not a conscious action. The women did not themselves clearly connect their anger with the auditor with their withdrawal from each other. "I don't know why," said the secretary, speaking of the decline of social activities. Yet they did withdraw and the withdrawal from each other was so conspicuous that all of them were aware of it.

That psychological distance is a critical factor in this problem was recognized by the cashier who asked, "I think that a supervisor should be more impersonal, don't you?" Her further spontaneous discussion about the appropriate balance between friendliness and impersonality, psychological distance in our terms, brings the problem clearly into the open as an important consideration in work relationships.

Components of Distance

We have chosen these two examples because they illustrate extremes of the concept of psychological distance, and throw into relief the dimensions of the concern with interpersonal relationships. Let us look at them more closely to discern some of the components of balanced distance.

The women in the first group spoke about friendships made on the job which did not "make any trouble with the company." They spoke repeatedly of the "wonderful group of girls." The management of the relationships, even that with the manager, lay largely in their own hands, although their supervisor, too, maintained certain controls of which they were aware. Obviously he would tolerate some behavior but not other behavior, and he would require that they do their work. In this situation of balanced distance, then, were feelings of *affection* and *control*.

The women in the second group spoke of the loss of affection and control. They no longer had the warmth with each other they had had before and they no longer had as much freedom to manage their own relationships. Something had happened to the relationship beyond their control. They spoke, furthermore, of having lost their *privacy*. They could not talk as freely with each other. They could not share "group secrets" for these were leaked to the boss, and he leaked even private secrets. Loss of balanced distance, in turn, made it difficult to gratify dependent needs in relationships with superiors and co-workers. Certainly they could not depend on the supervisor, and the growing distance among the women made it harder to maintain interdependence.

Affection, privacy, and *control* would appear to be components of balanced psychological distance. We cannot say at this point that these are the only components of distance or that any one is more important than another, but we can point to their presence. Included in the employee's side of the psychological contract with the organization is not merely the wish for friends. Rather, to the extent that we understand this aspect of it at this point, the psychological expectation is for the opportunity to balance one's relationships in such a way that he might have affection, privacy, and control in the degrees which are comfortable for him. After we came to our conception of affection, control, and privacy we learned of Schutz's (29) postulate of three interpersonal need areas which directly parallel our three "components." He considers, as we do, but in a wider context than work, how social situation and role requirements interact with individual needs along the three dimensions of inclusion, control, and affection.

THE CONTEXT OF DISTANCE

The effort to obtain a balanced psychological distance in terms of the components we have described takes place in a context bounded by three important points: one's fellow workers, his superiors, and the requirements of his task.

Peer Relationships

Colleagues at the same hierarchical level are usually able to obtain an optimal psychological distance from one another. This is certainly not to say that co-workers do not have difficulties at times because they become psychologically too close or too distant from each other. Peers, however, have numerous controls which they utilize naturally to balance distance. There is no contract which requires that co-workers like one another or communicate with each other except as is required for the job. For people who do not want to work closely with someone, there is a variety of avoidance techniques, including minimal communication, which permits them relative isolation. Where the requirements of the job do not limit the closeness of interaction, mutual choice tends to function effectively in most cases to permit psychologically satisfying relationships to develop.

Power Relationships

Any supervisor-subordinate relationship requires particular kinds of interaction not controlled solely by the parties involved. Regardless of task requirements, supervisors and subordinates inevitably are interdependent by the very nature of their power relationship.

There are certain inherent limits on the expression of feelings. The subordinate cannot freely express negative attitudes he may have toward his superior to the degree that he might to a co-worker. Similarly, the superior must control his expression of feeling toward his subordinate both about the subordinate himself and about others in the work situation. Just as the power relationship exerts pressures toward certain kinds of communication, it also demands certain restraints. The two parties can choose only to a limited degree how much they interact because their work together requires particular kinds of interaction.

The interaction of a supervisor with any given subordinate has meaning for all the rest of the employees. Other employees might accept the fact that two co-workers were extremely close. But, the interaction of a supervisor which is too close with any given employee, as we saw with the second group of women, is interpreted by others negatively as increasing the distance between themselves and the supervisor, and thereby violating the psychological contract. Every time employees mentioned such closeness in the interviews, they were also concerned about favoritism. Whenever a supervisor mentioned closeness, he expressed discomfort because of the way in which this might be regarded as favoritism. If favoritism implied that one received more affection than others, the result was that others got less.

In the experience of the writers, most people in positions of authority frequently wrestle with the question of how close they should get to subordinates. The problem often is expressed as, "Should we be on a first-name basis?" or "How much contact should there be among levels in the hierarchy outside of work?" or the concern of people with authority because their feeling of closeness to some person impedes their ability to make what they consider a wise decision. Each of these illustrates the pressures concerning distance which are experienced by both supervisory and subordinate personnel in their relationships to one another.

This concern with distance is understandable not only because of the already described issues which are relatively rational aspects of the supervisor-subordinate relationship, but also from a psychoanalytic point of view in terms of the irrational, symbolic, and less conscious significance of the supervisor-subordinate relationship. "The boss" is not only the person with influence over his subordinate. He is a figure whose authority makes him like a father and other authorities who have had influence and power in the life of the subordinate. Hence, expressions of either anger or affection from a supervisor can trigger at both unconscious and conscious levels unrealistic concerns transferred from earlier relationships.

Such factors, particularly, increase the demands made upon a supervisor at any level for mature and objective reaction to his subordinates. He plays a particularly critical role in providing the context for balanced distance in interpersonal relationships among his subordinates, in relationships between them and him, and in their relationships with other figures in authority.

The significance of the supervisory-subordinate relationship for balanced distance was evident in the two contrasting examples we have already used in this chapter. The reader will recall the anger of the second group of women, the decay of group cohesion and the loss of balanced distance as a result of the supervisor's behavior. This was in sharp contrast to the gratification of the first group of women whose supervisor maintained a more balanced distance which enabled them to establish and seek their own most comfortable relations. This distance did not mean that the supervisor was almost absent as was the case with the manager in Chapter IV. It was close enough to provide sufficient direction to permit employees to function easily in appropriate work situations and at the same time made it possible for the women to behave in ways akin to those of our criteria. In Fiedler's studies of interpersonal distance and task effectiveness (9), he demonstrates the detrimental effects of relationships which are too distant or too close, particularly the relationships of leaders. He found also that the context of the relationship was an important factor in determining what is balanced and appropriate interpersonal distance. Bennis, in a recent review of leadership theory and research (6), draws attention to the common task as a criterion against which leaders and subordinates can judge the suitability of the psychological distance between them.

Task Requirements

Task requirements set limits on closeness or distance, regardless of what is tolerable and comfortable for the individuals.

Considerable interdependence is required of members of a line crew. Crewmen referred frequently to the closeness with which they had to work. Safety alone required that the men be in touch with what each was doing. The men often said explicitly they needed to know the moods, strengths, and weaknesses of others on the crews. They emphasized that when they were not close to each other in this sense, accidents were likely to occur. They constantly worked together in small, tightly knit groups, facing new and dangerous situations. This intimacy in the work situation was reflected in the affection which developed, the necessity for knowing each other well, and the control which they felt must be exerted upon the total group and on individuals both by crewmen individually and by the foreman.

In contrast to the situation of the line crew were some work situations which required that the men be considerably isolated from each other. For example, the task for the men working in a large power plant was always that of control. The outsider felt the tremendous size of the operation. The plant itself was an extensive and complex maze of machinery. The relatively few men who controlled this vast power were widely separated from one another, spending their time checking on the dials to make sure that everything was under control. The noise limited speech.

Each person at work in the plant knew that every other worker, isolated from him as he might be in terms of verbal communication and even visibility, could cause problems. The way in which a person could cause an accident, and every worker was aware of the possibility of someone doing this, was illustrated in the following quotation from a researcher's diary: "One man told me, when discussing the effects of emotional upsets on personnel, that he once came to the plant mad and by mistake closed a switch which should have been opened but fortunately this was detected immediately. He commented that if the mistake hadn't been detected, the consequences would have been catastrophic."

On the other hand, the men were constantly doing a considerable amount of checking of machines and dials. The checking up, uncertainty as to who might be doing what, and the possible consequences of their doing the wrong thing, which were necessary aspects of the tasks in this location, tended to make for suspicion and distrust of others. A shift foreman exemplified the feeling: ". . . sometimes there's a little trouble when not enough is logged up from shift to shift. It makes you wonder what they did do, what they put in or what they tore up."

There was anxiety since something over which one had no direct control could get out of hand and cause one's destruction. An operator said:

> . . . A foreman ought to be where his men are and know exactly what is going on, especially in a power plant. A foreman could put you on a job somewhere taking a valve off, and you got ready to take the last bolt off and maybe you saw some steam coming out — if you got out of there okay that would be fine, but you might not be able to tell about it. Things like that can make you lose confidence. Somebody didn't shut off the pipe before you removed that valve . . . I always try to be pretty careful . . .

The men were interdependent whether they liked it or not. They had to, in some way, handle their concerns about the ever-present danger.

People who chose to remain in a situation like this probably had less need for close interpersonal relations than the linemen. However, pressures toward the kind of isolation described, and restriction of the opportunity for close and frequent contacts with others in the plant so that one could not get the information which was important to his well-being, tended to increase distance to uncomfortable limits even for some who were relative isolates. Beyond the factors which we have already mentioned, there was greater isolation in evening and midnight shifts when maintenance crews were not in the plant.

In some instances the men handled such psychological distance in ways which increased it further, leading to additional conflict. Unallayed fears contributed to suspicion and distrust. When the anger which developed out of the fantasies about what others might be doing, which in turn might cause one difficulties, could not be channeled usefully, it was directed sometimes toward the organization as a whole, sometimes toward the supervisor and sometimes toward fellow workers in the form of criticism and distrust.

A welder said of management:

On these working relations, I wonder if they want it to move smoothly. It seems to me sometimes they just stir people up to get more work out of them.

For some men in this plant and in similar plants, more constructive handling of distance was possible, despite the pressures toward isolation. Where communication was emphasized among personnel to compensate for their isolation, as in the form of active relations between supervisors and men, or where an employee had a relatively comfortable relationship with a particular supervisor, fears and distrust seemed to be lessened. The supervisory relationship frequently provided a channel for venting anxiety and anger, and for the development of bonds of security which compensated for some of the concerns. Faith in the capacity of supervisory personnel to maintain control over the various people with heavy responsibilities in the plant appeared to make up for the lack of specific knowledge about what the other man was doing.

In Perspective

The interrelationships of affection, privacy, and control in the context of peer relationships, power relationships, and task requirements, are illustrated by several quotations from a single crew. The first comment came from a third-year apprentice:

I lose my temper too much I know. When you first start working, it is hard to learn to calm down and keep calm. The critical time is your first year. I just used to get fouled up all the time. If you do that you get to stamping around and not thinking about what you're doing. A lineman's got to use his head all the time. He's got to know when to use horseplay and when to attend to his business. You don't want any horseplay up there on the pole but you've got to have a little fun on the job too.

. . . I think things like that make for good working conditions. That kidding around. But you have to know how to take it . . . I think this coffee break is a good deal. You get all the chattering done you're going to do otherwise on the job. And then you talk things over going in to work . . .

[Talking of the crew foreman] he never loses his head. He thinks of his men all the time . . . his men come first. He's always watching to prevent your doing something you'd be sorry you did. He never brings his home troubles to work either. That's a bad thing in a foreman or a man. A foreman who does that injures his crew . . .

Another member of the same crew talked about the importance of keeping emotions in check for working closely with and being interdependent with others in the crew:

You've got to give and take. Sometimes you feel you're kinda getting the dirty end of things, but you've got to overlook them. It might be your own fault. You've got to learn what's going on around you. You depend on your pole buddy and you've got to help him because you may need him to help you sometime.

Learning to work with people and to get along were the most important aspects of the job, he thought.

Everyone has their ups and downs on the job . . . things differ a lot from crew to crew. Each foreman does things in a different way . . . even on the same pole two guys may start up the pole differently and you can look at the differences as you see them climb.

The mutual affection which developed in work was reflected in his comment about how working out major problems led to closeness.

When they have a storm the guys work extra hard. I like to work with a bunch of guys. When you work along with the guys for a long time you learn to like them and they learn to like you . . . if I get sick some days I damn sight would rather be at work and that's the kind of job to have . . . guys that can't work along with a bunch of fellows don't stay long around on the job . . . If a guy gets riled up all the fellows start kidding him. He's not going to buck everybody so he calms down . . . Everything goes on around the foreman. He's been here longer and everyone looks to him . . . the foreman is there to keep things going along and no one is better than anyone else on the crew.

The foreman of the crew, of which these two men were members, described the several aspects of distance in work:

I don't like to work by myself. That's one thing I like about this place here . . . [He preferred the contact with one crew rather than the demands which would be made upon him were he to be in charge of several crews.] Out here I've got one crew and I work with these boys every day . . . I sure like it here.

The foreman should be one of the men. He should be one of the boys instead of out on a limb. Who the foreman is has a hell of a lot to do with working relations. If he is just one of the boys and works along with them, things will go along good . . . the crew will all work good unless someone is not feeling good. Whenever we have any trouble, someone has a bad cold or back trouble. Usually the fellows will josh each other but if a fellow isn't feeling right he won't josh any more . . .

It's like I said before — if you're going to be one of the boys rather than superior to them it will be much better for you in running the crew. I let them go along their own way but when they get too wrong I suggest changes and they agree. That's the way we work it . . . they're all good men. You're just there if they need you to work along with them.

The foreman was on intimate terms with his crew, yet he managed to maintain a distance which enabled him to use his authority. He played poker with them and submitted to a lot of kidding during the day, but he never lost sight of the reason they were together — the job. Such a focus put his relationship in perspective, and particularly counteracted tendencies toward too much closeness. However the feeling for him on the part of the crew members was warm and trusting. They respected his judgment and would quietly ask him an opinion about how something should be done. Sometimes this was only the desire for his approval for the use of a technique they already knew. The atmosphere in the crew work situation, to researchers who observed the crew, seemed to be smoother when the foreman was there than it was when someone else was running the crew.

In these excerpts we saw how the work itself made certain demands upon the men. The particular way these demands and pressures toward closeness were handled was, of course, stamped with the style of the particular crew. Kidding and mutual joshing, seen widely among the crews, served the purpose of draining off hostile feelings and thereby keeping tensions from building up.

Whatever method of working together characterized a particular crew style, however leadership was handled, or how closely the men interacted, they were faced with certain realities. Each to some degree placed his life in the hands of others. A slip by one man who might be preoccupied with a personal problem could be dangerous, so all crew members were sensitive to the moods and emotions of other members. There were obvious needs for spontaneous, affectionate interchange which had to be controlled in some way. There were times for play and fun. There were times for seriousness and minimum spontaneity, such as when men were near "hot" wires. These times were recognized from experience which the crews had had, and from direction by senior members, foremen in particular.

The apprentice indicated that the danger of the work itself forced him to exert controls over his own behavior, helping him during the particularly crucial first year to incorporate controls as part of his identity. Controls were reinforced by the foreman, who did not, however, "breathe down their necks." He did permit them to play, still in controlled fashion, when it was appropriate to play. He did not invade their privacy with his own problems, but he kept an ear open for their problems which would help him understand their needs better. It was striking how the apprentice recognized that if the foreman were to bring his problems to the job, he would "injure his crew."

The lineman reminded us that affection means to be helpful and to accept the occasional hostility of the other person. Without affection, he said, a person could not remain a member of the crew. Survival on the job required it. The continuity of relationships was apparently also required for a continuing source of affection and control. The foreman, in his judgment, kept an appropriate distance from the crew because, despite his talk of being "one of the boys," he distributed his own affection evenly among them.

In a sense, the story of these men might be summarized as, "We work very closely. We have to. This is gratifying, but the same pressures toward gratifying closeness also can lead to excessive closeness if we are not careful. Along with the affection we have for one another, there is anger, and we have to develop ways of handling it. That way we don't destroy ourselves. Each of us has a responsibility in this. We have to accept the importance of some of our personal problems since it can be dangerous to impose these on others during periods of crisis. We have to welcome the control that other members of the crew give us."

The Broader Context

Relationships and task requirements occurred in a broader setting which had sociocultural and geographic characteristics. These also became factors affecting the balancing of psychological distance. For example, some company operations were more isolated from the rest, particularly if they were also isolated from cities and towns. People lived and worked so closely together that they had to take steps to assure affection, privacy, and control in directions quite different from those taken by the group of women described at the beginning of the chapter. Said a man in one such location:

> The less you visit back and forth, the better. It's not good to get too chummy . . . We go out and visit, sure, but we don't make a practice of visiting anybody steady.

People helped each other, but they found it necessary to drive to communities away from the work location where there could be relief from the continual proximity of work and home. Supervisors became more keenly sensitive about behaving in ways which might stimulate fears in their subordinates about favoritism. They did not visit the homes of employees. Customs developed which restricted socialization, emphasizing the desirability of public interactions rather than extensive and special private interactions. It was acceptable to "talk over the fence" or while two men were mowing their lawns, but not for one to enter the home of another.

There were, of course, many other situational factors which tended to press people more closely together or to pull them farther from each other. We have not constructed an exhaustive list, but rather have illustrated the nature of the concern with distance and some of the forces related to it.

The task of obtaining a balanced distance in relationships to others is not only affected by many forces, but it is also a reciprocal and continuous process. Balanced distance is not something, like a diploma, which one attains and then keeps. It must constantly be sought and maintained.

SOME EFFECTS OF OPTIMAL DISTANCE AND GRATIFICATIONS

We can see how the process of establishing and maintaining comfortable interpersonal relations at work affects the opportunities for people to behave in ways indicative of good mental health. For example, the concern with balancing psychological distance is related most closely to having a wide variety of sources of gratification. The first group of women took pleasure in the small events of the working day. Those who wished to socialize enjoyed their friends and their social activities with friends. Those who did not wish to socialize were free to enjoy whatever other aspects of their work gave them pleasure. In the second group, the women were angry that they had lost sources of gratification, particularly social gratification. They found themselves more constricted, "working only for the money."

We do not mean to imply that every woman in the first group had a wide variety of sources of gratification and therefore had good mental health, nor that none of the women in the second group had any sources of gratification and therefore were mentally ill. Rather, balanced distance in the first group made it possible for those women to have a wider variety of gratifications than they might otherwise have had, and to the extent that they actually obtained more gratification, they were that much healthier.

That they were healthier, at least for that period of time the researchers were in touch with them, was reflected in their spontaneous willingness to help each other when one or another felt particularly burdened. They were able to treat each other as individuals — listening to the other when necessary, welcoming travelers from trips, recognizing the anxiety of the new manager and assuring him of their support.

The second group was an angry group, too far apart now for either gratification from each other or to be able to treat others as individuals. The climate was now more each woman for herself and the resulting work atmosphere was characterized by the word "uproar."

With the line crew, in addition to the gratification obtained from the supervisor and other crew members, balanced distance made possible controls over immaturity and impulsiveness. Thus the apprentice said he need no longer "get to stamping around and not thinking." Controls enabled him to be flexible in difficult situations. A crewman specifically pointed out the need to recognize individual differences and to treat people on the basis of these differences. Unlike the second group of women, these men were not forced so far apart that they had to withdraw from each other, thereby losing some of the ability to treat others as individuals and the flexibility to cope with stress which stems from group cohesiveness.

Schopenhauer told a story which Freud later quoted (10). Two porcupines faced the cold night. In order to warm themselves they had to come closer to each other. The closer they came, the more they stuck one another with their quills. Their problem was how to get the most heat with the least pain. How close could they get without hurting each other? This is the story of the problem of balanced distance.

CHAPTER VI

CHANGE

As in most other companies, many of Midland's processes were being automated. A new unit was being installed in a power plant which would almost double its generating capacity. The unit was nearly ready to go on the line. The method of handling the boilers, turbines, and auxiliary equipment was radically different from the system which had existed in the plant up to that time. Before, operating crews were split into three groups. One group fired boilers, another group operated auxiliary equipment such as fuel lines and switches, while a third group handled controls on the turbines and generators, together with the connections to the transmission lines, through a huge substation located between the plant and the river.

In the new unit, a smaller number of employees operated the interlocking complex of equipment systems by remote control. The firebox was seen, not through a peephole on the face of the furnace, but on a television screen. Instead of wrestling with a giant valve to regulate fuel or water, the operator flicked a switch or turned a dial, and electronic controls did the work. Instead of the heat, noise, and dirt on the plant floor, the work environment for operators and maintenance personnel now was a long, coolly lighted room, dominated by a gigantic control panel which was a maze of dials, colored lights, and switches. The roar of the plant was reduced to a hum; people were summoned not by the siren heard in the old plant but by a muted telephone bell.

Only a small number of the employees worked in the new unit. Most continued to work in the old environment, but there was movement from one environment to the other, particularly by maintenance people.

The plant was undergoing another kind of change, from an older generation of employees to a younger one. Some of the older men had worked in the plant from the time it was built; some had even helped build it. A number of others had come into the plant during the preceding decade. The older group was about to retire. The younger group was anticipating moving into vacancies created by their departure and by the growth of the plant.

The growth of the demand for power had required that the company expand its generating capacity, and the anticipated increasing demand meant that for some years to come the company would have to keep increasing its production. Furthermore, the efficiency of automated techniques and the rapidity of their evolution meant that the methods of plant operation not only would change, but also would continue to change with each expansion. The company, in addition, was a partner with other privately owned utilities in an experimental project to study the possibilities of atomic energy as a fuel for generating electricity. Should this venture prove successful, further changes would be in the offing though these were not likely for several years.

In sum, the company had to change the operation of its generating processes. Implicit in its psychological contract with the employees was the expectation that they, too, would change, for it was they who would have to operate this and other new units. All companies must necessarily presume a certain amount of flexibility on the part of employees. The company acted on the assumption that, given training to familiarize themselves with the new operations, the men would take them over. The company was also governed by the formal contract whose seniority provisions might require that at least some of the newer, easier jobs be given to men with the longest seniority. The casual observer might readily assume that everyone would want to work in the newer, most pleasant unit. There were, however, three different kinds of reactions.

One group of employees interviewed (we may call them the Elders because they were preponderantly from the older and most senior part of the work force) seemed to adopt as their slogan: "Preserve the status quo." Aproximately a quarter of the employees interviewed saw life in the plant this way. They were people who had "grown up" with the plant and prided themselves on long service and the know-how which stemmed from that service. They felt that their capacities were overtaxed by changes in plant technology, but their resentment was tempered somewhat by their gratitude for the care and consideration which they felt the company had shown them in their later years.

Another group of employees, young in age and seniority, seemed always to be saying in one way or another, "Times have changed." They were eager for the new skills and new experiences which the additional plant capacity involved. Their impatience stemmed from the feeling that "management," meaning those with whom they came in contact, and the "old timers" were refusing to recognize or admit that times had changed. These men we labeled the Heirs.

A third group included people of various ages and seniority levels but seemed to be composed mostly of those between the Elders and Heirs in terms of age and seniority. They were acutely aware of the transition from the old to the new that was going on in the plant, but had not yet "placed their bets." Their position could be summarized in the slogan, "Wait and See." They were the Neutrals, ready to concur with the Elders if traditional policies in the plant should survive the introduction of the new unit and other changes, ready to follow the Heirs if a new point of view should triumph.

The differences among the three groups were highlighted by their views on training. Each handled its insecurities in the face of changing technology in keeping with its particular perspective.

The Elders, for the most part, elected not to get involved with the new unit. Said one,

> They've got me down here running these old units that aren't on automatic. The need for my job might be expired when they get all this construction and everything done. I'd just as leave be retired before that time comes.

The Heirs, for their part, criticized "management" for what they viewed to be failure to provide adequate training. One comment was typical:

> I can't understand when they have a big plant like this with all this money tied up in equipment why the training program is not too good . . . They would save millions of dollars, maybe, if people were properly trained. They would save ruining a lot of equipment.

The Neutrals mentioned training as a need, but averred "It's management's problem."

These categories, like any classifications, are oversimplifications. As abstractions, they fail to take into account individual differences and many other factors in and outside of the plant. For understanding some of the meanings of this change, however, these categories will serve.

PATTERNS OF REACTION
Increasing Separation

The Elders generally had an eighth grade education, sometimes less, and they were keenly aware of the fact that this, which originally had made little difference in their employment, was now a limitation. When they had first come to work, many had come for just a job. They had acquired most of their skills on the job and had defined their adult occupational roles on the basis of these skills and their seniority in the plant. The tenuousness of their original psychological contracts was reflected in their comments about the meaning of electricity when they first went to work. Many had joined the company when electricity was still a novelty and a few could remember when it was said that electricity would not last. According to the psychological contract, as they had come to view it and as it had been carried out over the years, they would be able to continue to use skills acquired on the job, based on manual dexterity and mechanical knowledge, and to have increasing security as well as job status with seniority.

In the course of their long years of service, they had also developed relationships with each other based on status, skill, and personal preference. In these relationships they had evolved certain balances in their psychological distance from each other. Each knew to what extent he could depend on the other and how close he wanted to be to the other. They had had the same superintendent for some years with whom their relationship was not particularly close.

When the company had been forced by economic and technological circumstances to change its expectations, the Elders experienced the change as a violation of the psychological contract because it represented to them both a *loss* and a *demand*. The older men had been operators or mechanics for years. The shift from the old to the new method of operation required of the Elder not merely the acquisition of new skills, but a complete shift in his own self-image. The identity he had established for himself began to be blurred.

The Elders would be increasingly less able to do what they had done before. Their experience, once so valuable, gave them little to fall back on, for now they would have to deal with more complex electronic equipment. Having lost the value of much of their experience and some of the previously respected image of themselves, they had limited ability to meet the added stress when it was, in effect, "demanded" that they acquire new skills. In short, they had lost much of their ability to respond to the stress situation. As they saw it, they were being asked to do something they were not prepared to do, emotionally as well as intellectually. Instead of becoming skilled by identification with an older, more skilled man, over a long period of time, now they were asked to learn quickly through instruction.

At a time when their dependency needs would be most acute — when traditional patterns of behavior were to be disrupted — there were few sources of personal support. New opportunities, better working conditions, and greater efficiency were being provided. But the Elders saw these changes (not necessarily consciously) as deprivation and as making demands of them which were not previously in the psychological contract. To complicate matters further, they could not help but be aware of the Heirs, who would soon not only displace them physically but who also even now were about to displace them psychologically by threatening to take over the more complex job roles. Such displacement would mean loss of the status which had been so laboriously acquired by seniority.

Furthermore, the structure of the old work group, as they had known it, was now broken up. They would once again have to establish new balances in distance. Some younger men, instead of being their juniors, would assume senior occupational roles. There would be changes in the amount of contact they would have with each other and, in the new-found quietness of the control room, in the degree of closeness possible in those contacts. In short, they would lose not only some kinds of personal relationships, but also valued work skills and regular work routines, and at the same time have to re-establish all three. They were threatened with a wholesale loss of gratifications.

So the task of learning the new controls and assuming the new responsibilities was complicated by the hostile feelings which were aroused. To these feelings were added the fears of being blamed and criticized should something go wrong. As one man noted:

The fellow I'm working with now, it's kinda hard for him to get onto the new controls. On the old equipment, he knew from experience what to do, but this is all new . . . There are parts of this that many of us don't know how to do but if we couldn't do the job, they would place the blame on us and it would be up to us to clear ourselves.

Some avoided the possible failure in working with the new equipment by refusing promotion or transfer, thus defining for themselves a much too narrow range of limitations and restricting their own productive contributions.

On this new unit . . . they just show it to you once and then they expect you to know it. You've got to catch on quick. We've got some trained men but they aren't working on the new unit. They say they'd rather stay on the old unit.

The company had anticipated the need for training the men to use the new equipment. The men themselves were aware of their need for training, an awareness heightened by the difficulties of some of the people assigned to operate the complex equipment through the seniority system. The desire for training was thus a legitimate one. The men did need to be trained to handle the new equipment, and the company recognized that need. But behind the request for more training, we inferred a plea to be understood. It was as if the Elders were saying to management, "You don't understand how weak and inadequate I feel in the face of this change. You are demanding more of me despite the fact that I am less capable of responding to the demand for having suffered a deprivation. I can't fall back on what I knew before and there is no one who will help me deal with this experience, for which I never bargained." The psychological distance between the Elders, their colleagues and their superiors was becoming wider. As a result, the Elders saw themselves and the organization growing further and further apart.

The organization was expanding, becoming more complex and more powerful. They were becoming physically and psychologically less powerful. Characteristically, they withdrew into their own psychological shells, to hold on as long as they could to that which was left of the old ways and to nurse their anger and frustration that the psychological contract had been violated.

Joint Decline

Parenthetically, and by way of contrast, let us look at the experience of another group of Elders in another plant. The company knew that some of the power plants "inherited" from merged companies were an economic disadvantage. For this reason, Midland was converting the smaller and older plants from continuous operations to "stand-by" status. The least efficient boilers and generators were shut down. When an employee in one of these plants terminated or retired, his job duties were often divided among those who remained. For example, operators began to do some maintenance work, and superintendents did more record-keeping, replacing clerks or helpers. Yet the stand-by plants were still vital to company operations. When a heat wave boosted the electric load for air conditioning or a thunderstorm temporarily knocked out a transformer at a major plant, the smaller, older plants were available to swing into full operation and thus maintain continuous service.

In the smaller plants, most of the work groups were composed of older employees who had spent many years together at the same location. Most of them had not long to go until retirement. Thus the conversion of such a plant to stand-by status was of special psychological significance because it came at a time when the worker was wondering about his value to the organization. People in the older plants spoke directly of this meaning in their interviews. A superintendent of one of the stand-by plants said:

We're to the point now where, I hate to admit it, but this plant could run by itself.

Others talked about the conversion to stand-by status like this:

I like it better on stand-by but at my age that's natural. If I were younger now, I'd rather be operating and have a chance to progress, work up . . . Of course, for us old fellows it makes for a nice thing because the work is lighter.

Here there was direct confrontation of the fact that a man's working life as well as the life of his plant was drawing to an end.

A senior plant operator pointed out that there were some elements in the situation, in addition to the lighter work, which made it possible to accept one's own limitations and capacities, despite "obsolescence" of oneself. Among these additional factors were an understanding attitude by management and the guarantee of job security, an important element in the psychological contract.

> Mr. ———— was very considerate of the older employees. We had a man working here who got to the place where he couldn't do anything at all. Mr. ———— said that a man has a job as long as he can stay on his feet . . . You know and I know that they could lay me off tomorrow and get more work per dollar out of a younger man. Of course, all of the experience is to an old man's advantage.

For men like this, there was no contractual violation despite evident change. Legitimate dependency was still recognized and supported, and the older employees were still able to maintain a balanced distance between themselves and others in the organization. They were not called upon to change their relationships to each other or to their supervision. Their interdependence was maintained. The changes in that part of the organization in which they worked were congruent with the changes within themselves. There was an experience of loss, but there was no additional demand. In fact, the loss was tempered by decreasing demand. Both plant and men could be described as obsolescent, yet they were still important and valuable to the organization.

Joint Growth

To return to our original example, for the Heirs there was a quite different psychological contract than that held by the Elders. Few of the young workers remembered the depression as keenly as did the older men; they placed somewhat less emphasis on financial security. All were better educated than the Elders. Their education gave them greater confidence about what their future might hold. The newer men had come to the company during a period of rapid expansion of electric service. They not only knew electricity was here to stay, but also that its horizons were unlimited. Their initial relationship to the electrical business was not one of "maybe," as it had been for the Elders, but one in which they anticipated company expansion, greater technological training, and a continuing affiliation with the electrical generating business.

The Heirs experienced the new demands which the changing contract placed on them, but they had no accompanying feeling of loss. Many were still defining their adult occupational identities for themselves. They had not yet set goals for specific jobs and places in the organization. They did not have to give up cherished self-images or status. They had no positions of power based on seniority, which might define the limits of psychological distance, therefore they were more free to control their own distances from the others. They did not see the changes as affecting that freedom. Furthermore, learning from books or in a classroom was less foreign to them. For them, this change was part of the psychological contract.

The situation of the Heirs could be viewed as the "mirror image" of the experiences reported by older people in the older plants. Here again, there was a parallel between organizational process and personal life circumstances. Younger employees saw in the more complex technology and growth of the plant a preview of their own work life history. Their psychological contract called for increasing their work competence and broadening their work experience. They would continue to demand more and more training, and to be critical of what they got; for them, there would almost never be enough. Given continuous training, both legitimate dependency and balanced distance could be maintained because both men and organization would grow together and the changing contract would not be considered to be violated.

We have spoken so far of three reactions to changes in the psychological contract brought about by the company's changing expectations. We say "the company's changing expectations" rather than "management's changing expectations" because in these instances the survival of the company would have required the changes regardless of any given management.

In the first example, the Elders experienced the changes as a violation of the psychological contract because they suffered both psychological loss and increased psychological demand. They felt that their interdependence with the company was considerably less than it had been, and that the psychological distance between themselves and others had increased to uncomfortable proportions. They saw themselves as having to cope alone with the demands of changing technology. They had not only lost many gratifications, but also they had become less flexible in their reactions to this stress. They withdrew from the work situation as best they could. They narrowed their perceptions of their own abilities and stereotyped their view of both the Heirs and management.

In the second example, the Elders remained psychologically at one with the company because the company's changing expectations were congruent with their declining capacities. The changes did not interfere with meeting legitimate dependency needs or alter the distance between men in the company. There was joint coping with change. There was little loss of gratifications. Their perception of their abilities and productivity was governed by reality considerations, for example, physical changes.

In the third example, the Heirs experienced the company's changing expectations as in keeping with their own expanding personal horizons. Despite increasing gratifications, they experienced some stress, for they stereotyped both management and the Elders. They did, however, maintain a realistic view of their assets and saw themselves as increasing their contribution to the organization.

There were at least two other kinds of reactions at Midland to alterations in the company's side of the psychological contract. Both occurred over a longer period of time than the previous examples and in both the individual concerned mentioned no figure in the larger organization with whom he could identify himself.

Because of the extended time span, there was not the dramatic crisis seen in earlier examples. One reaction was to feel psychologically left behind or deserted by the company, the other was psychologically to leave the company behind and to invest more of one's feelings elsewhere.

Being Left Behind

A division manager serves as an example for the first. Speaking of the executive of a merged company who had made a place for him in the business, he said:

I think that all young fellows are swayed by personal relations they have with people and my relationship with this executive was of that kind . . . And I like community work. This is what finally decided me.

Almost immediately he was put in charge of company operations in the town which was now the headquarters of the division he headed. He said that his predecessor was a "good operator" but,

. . . had no conception of how to deal with the public. I had ideas about how to create greater customer acceptance for the power and light business . . . I stepped in with zeal to do the job.

Early promotion gave rein to ideas and zeal. After the dissolution of the holding companies, the image they had left in the public mind remained to be changed. The manager wanted to prove himself and his company worthy of public confidence.

His years in the community, his membership and leadership in civic organizations, and participation in community projects, all had been devoted, in his eyes, to building an identity for himself and an image of the company as a responsible and contributing part of the community.

Increasingly he was the company in his community. Over the years man and company became closer. His roots in both company and community grew deeper.

His part of the psychological contract had been for personalized service. His interest in service, the executive who became his early identification model, and rapid movement into an executive position all contributed to an early definition of his adult occupational role. He enjoyed handling situations where he was able to solve the customer's problems. But now he could no longer do so in the same personal way. He began to lose many of his former sources of gratification. He could adjust the payment dates of bills only within very narrow limits. He was less able to treat his customers as individuals. Thus, he might think he is seen by the customer as the heartless bureaucrat rather than the Main Street merchant he would like to be:

> We ought to be like the clothing company down the street here. Say you go in there and buy a shirt and necktie and charge it. We'll give you from 30 to 60 days to pay your bill. You have faith in people like that who will pay their bills . . . In contrast to this, people come in here [to the utility company] with their money and say, "I'd better get in here before you shut my lights off."

In addition to central billing, now required by increasing growth and machine bookkeeping operations, which limited his flexibility to adjust bills, the manager had experienced increasing specialization of other operations. One of the manager's subordinates described what had happened:

> Years ago when the utilities were smaller and the manager used to do the whole damned thing — he was the engineer, the meter reader, the collector, and the manager. Since the company and the industry have gotten so big, they have to specialize now. Some of the managers who have been here a long time don't realize that. They try to do everything.

The increasing specialization led the manager to comment: "Shaw looks on the manager as an office boy." Faced with these events which seemed to diminish the value of his assets and increase his limitations, he wondered if his contributions to the company were appreciated. He felt that the company should give some tangible evidence that he was still a valued member of the organization:

I do think that the guys who get out and work like hell, overtime, without recompense, ought to be recognized in some fashion. Maybe just in terms of a pat on the back, I don't know.

The changes had brought his increased status and power, and opportunities for better service, but the psychological contract in the new merged organization was no longer of his making. Now he was more distant psychologically from top management and from customers as well. Policies and procedures could not substitute for his former close relationship with his superiors, nor could greater responsibility and more service opportunities compensate for his feeling of having lost his proximity to the customer. Not to fulfill the image which the contract had previously fostered left him feeling that he was an office boy. Curiously, had he not lost distance from top management and the customers at the same time, he might just as well have felt he was a more important executive, for the higher an executive rises, the less detail, supposedly, is his lot.

We must not forget, incidentally, that every man must come to terms with his own chronological and physiological changes. His view of these changes necessarily colors his view of other changes. Every man must recognize in mid-life that he will not be able to fulfill all his dreams and ambitions. Disappointment in self can easily be displaced onto a company, particularly when the psychological contract appears to promise so much. In some respects, at least, this compounds the problem of the manager.

From an original psychological contract calling for community work, in which both parties concurred, the psychological contract on the company's side had changed to require of him that he be a boss, a defender of the company, and finally the company personified. There were other changes in the psychological contract: merger, growth, more efficient control systems. These were on the company's side alone; he had not seen them as part of the contract which he had undertaken. The organization's requirements for profits and cost control, together with the manager's functions as an administrator, often prevented his providing the personal service which he had contracted to give. Here again is the concurrent experience of loss and demand.*

"Leaving" the Company

The final kind of reaction to change was typified by an outside districtman. He explained how he felt about the changes he had seen during his company service:

> I've worked here 23 years. These companies do get too large. You lose your personal contact. After all, I'm just a farm boy. I like things that way . . . The bigger they get, the worse they get . . . It's the same as the government. It all gets very impersonal. You don't deal with people any more, just with departments.

As his relationships with the company began to be less rewarding, he sought more of his gratifications in the community. In contrast with the manager above, he made his main investments in the community. Almost all of his time with the company had been spent in the little town which was his base of operations. In that town, he got married and reared his family. He was recognized as a community leader. The company had expected that he would advance to greater responsibility. Many times the company tried to transfer him, but he insisted on staying where he was:

> They wanted me to move over to another town as the manager. But I know everyone here. My wife belongs to the clubs. We enjoy it.

When he started on the job, few had electricity. Now there were 1,300 customers — most of them the districtman knew personally. As more people used electricity, his own importance increased.

During these years the company grew. A merger occurred. His

---

* Warren Bennis comments on this point: "There is something tragic here. For it seems that (such members of) middle management . . . learned their lessons so well that they couldn't adapt to tomorrow's needs. This is truly tragic and generalizable to many other companies, particularly technically based ones. With the speed of obsolescence here and with the contract specifying 'security,' then the older men who 'never made it' are put into a position where they are penalized and punished for overlearning yesterday's lessons too well — and not being capable of adapting to tomorrow's. (And worse, not being able to leave.)"

district and its division became part of a power grid stretching over hundreds of miles. "The company," which he once viewed as almost a home town institution, he now perceived as something big and almost foreign. The company expected him to become more businesslike as it was required to do. Occasionally he saw it as the source of demands which strained the customer relationships (or increased his psychological distance from customers) in which the districtman had invested his working years.

I hate to cut people's lights off. After all, I know them all around here. A lot of them have had hard luck . . . In the old days . . . if you thought they were deserving you'd carry them another month. We carried some five, six, seven, eight months.

Like the division manager above, his original psychological contract was for security and to render personal service to his friends. But unlike the division manager, he had no authority figure with whom to identify. As a result, he chose to remain a farmer among farmers. Despite his wish to do so, he never really established close ties with the company as an organization. His power to use the organization for his friends had diminished, so his guilt increased as he interpreted some of his official actions to be unfair to them. With increasing guilt came increasing anger toward the company. That was not the psychological contract as he understood it. Despite his increasing importance in the community, which the company had made possible, changing company practices now seemed to curb his freedom to act on the company's behalf. For him, as for the manager, service meant what he personally did, not what the company provided its customers in more consistent and reliable electric service.

Despite a protest to the contrary, he still yearned for an identification figure and closer ties to the organization:

Me, I don't give a damn, but a lot of the boys do like to have the president come around once in awhile. I mean the chairman of the board, the big wheel. If he comes out and pats you on the back and says you did a good job, that makes you feel pretty good too . . . A lot of people have the idea that the chairman of the board and the president own the company. There's not one in ten agrees with me on this, but they're in a tough spot. They've got to make the stockholders happy and keep employees halfway satisfied too . . . People ought to know that the chairman has a job and works just like we do. They can throw him out like anyone at the annual meeting. Of course they probably wouldn't but they could.

He wanted to have powerful identification figures, but they were too far away from him. His cry was almost plaintive, "Boss, where are you, why don't you come and see what I have done?" As a reasonable man, he knew the boss had his job to do, and that he, too, was only an employee, but this did not satisfy his need. Apparently he tried to minimize its importance by equating the boss with himself. So he found his gratifications among his friends. There he assuaged his own dependency needs by taking care of them. He was thus able to replace sources of psychological support which he had lost.

Without an identification figure, and not having come early to a management position, his advancement aspirations were limited. Once his investment in the community became paramount, then that with the company was secondary. He had no need to move up. This strength in the community made his needs different from those of the manager whose psychological contract was still primarily with the company.

It was because his relationship had developed with the community that the loss of the company as part of himself was not as painful as it might have been. The lost personal relationships of the once-small company were replaced by those among his friends. With each passing year the community ties became stronger.

In these five reactions to organizational change, we have examined more closely than in previous chapters some of the company's expectations which were part of its side of the psychological contract. We have seen that when the company changes the contract in such a way as to fail to gratify previously accepted dependency needs, or upsets the balance in psychological distance, while at the same time failing to cope with the changes jointly with the employees, various forms of hostility and withdrawal occur in response to the new demands which are made, but when change takes place without such disruptions, it is not experienced as a contractual violation.

Loss of a Leader

These changes were essentially mechanical and operational. There is another major organizational change which is more difficult to deal with, the loss of a leader. Although such a change may be viewed as simply a personal loss having little to do with the psychological contract with the organization, it is as a matter of psychological fact part of the company's side of the contract. Unconsciously, such a loss is perceived by subordinates as a deprivation and their reactions carry overtones of rejection and depression.

In chapter I we noted that the postwar years had been a time of rapid turnover in Midland management ranks. A large number of top and middle management people — vice presidents, division managers, local managers, and staff specialists — were reaching retirement age at the same time. The replacement needs as a result of retirements were accelerated by other forces: death or incapacitating illness in some positions; and company growth, which required the expansion of management forces or the appointment to management jobs of people who were better equipped than their predecessors to cope with increased work loads and greater responsibility.

Many of the departing leaders were closely identified by company people with the merged older organizations, now segments of the new organization, in which they had spent their working careers. Their passing, therefore, was symbolic of and associated with other kinds of changes going on simultaneously in the company: changes in organizational structure and altered technology. These associations came to the fore in these comments from one of the younger members of company management:

You'll find the influence of Dick Cole [an executive who had retired] everywhere you go north of Raleigh . . . one thing was you could call him at any hour of the day or night, tell him your troubles, and get an answer. You might not like the answer but you would get an answer . . . He probably drove more miles than anybody else in the company. Here, I suppose, he was in three or four times a month . . . You don't get that now . . . I think the thing we miss most is the personal contact between management and us. Our only contact is when we go to Shaw and go in and see the president. Most of them feel the way I do. You hate to go in and bother him. Not that he wouldn't take the time, but he has plenty of work to keep him busy. Maybe you just want to visit with him. It wouldn't amount to a hill of beans but you'd like to talk things over.

A substation inspector grumbled:

The way I see it . . . You've got to have someone there in Nash [the division headquarters] who can give yes and no answers . . . Cole had that. That's the way we like to run it . . .

As the comments above indicated, Cole was viewed by subordinates variously as the ambassador from the northern area to the headquarters of the company, as the defender of the division's interests against "encroachment" by Shaw, and as the personification of the company to people under his jurisdiction. "If we needed something you could bet your bottom dollar that if he had to stop it later there had been a helluva roar about it in Shaw first." All of these perceptions led people in the northern area to share the image of the man who commented, "We consider Nash (the location of Cole's office) as the head of the company."

The loss of the protecting fatherly figure of Cole came at a time of increasing emphasis on efficiency and cost control, and therefore of increasing demands upon everyone in the division. His going was interpreted by some employees as an increasing domination of division operations by headquarters. As a line crew veteran expressed it, "When Mr. Cole retired, we were left out in the cold." Thus, the loss of a leader in the organization led to feelings of being rejected. These feelings then colored the interpretation of directives from headquarters concerning operations. One example was an order from Shaw requiring a reduction in overtime hours worked by certain crews. The linemen's view was put into words by one of the foremen:

We've got this economy drive now. I don't know what they are gonna do . . . They think we should put another crew out and chop overtime off. The way I see it, they aren't saving a dime . . . cause you've got to hold these good men up to get the work done. They're talking about calling in a contractor to string some wire. I can't see that. We can string the same wire for half as much. If they're gonna spend the money anyway, why not give it to the guys here?

With the loss of leaders go feelings of being deserted. Though a man may be happy for whatever good fortune requires his friends to leave, there is sorrow and regret when they do so. The more powerful the departing person, the more support that has been demanded of him, the greater the feeling of rejection when he leaves.

That was how it was with Dick Cole. For those in the northern part of the organization, the psychological contract involved a relationship with Dick Cole. When Cole retired, the men felt they were deserted, that no one was left to care. Unconsciously they were angry with Cole for having "deserted" them, but who can be angry with a man they viewed as being so good? They then had to turn their anger toward themselves: "They think we're no good. We're not worth caring about. The company would rather have others than reward us," was the feeling tone of the last quotation.

Almost every word from headquarters could then be viewed as another threat. Suddenly the agent of the company through whom dependency needs had been met most effectively was no longer there. In their anger with themselves and the company, the men were resistant and resentful.

Again a situation of change was characterized by both loss and demand. Given both circumstances, it was difficult for the men to deal flexibly with the change. When they reacted by depreciating themselves and attributing hostility to the company, they deprived themselves, at least temporarily, of some of their work gratifications.

Change — It's Wonderful

"More often than not, tomorrow will be better than yesterday. Today is already so much better that it holds out a promise of a better tomorrow." This theme occurred frequently among older men who had been with the company through much of its history. It was typified by a truck driver of many years experience. He commented with pride on his truck. Though it was a ton and a half, it could set up to forty-foot poles.

Things have changed in the company, he said, they used to have thirty and thirty-five foot poles but the truck they had wasn't big enough to set anything over a thirty. It used to be a thirty was a nice-sized pole. Now they won't set a transformer on anything hardly less than a forty.

His original psychological contract merely called for a job in his home town. He began by digging holes for poles. After this he went to power plant work, then to the line crew for many years. As his physical powers waned he returned to the power plant and from there went to a storeroom. Now, by his own preference he was back on the truck.

For each of his changing needs corresponding changes of jobs were possible in the company. But change was not limited to shift in jobs and better equipment. Speaking of the managers under whom he had worked, he observed,

. . . with these younger managers it seems to go along smoother. This [local manager] is a prince of a fellow. These young boys they're getting are good. I guess when you get older, you get more set in your ways. I know that's true with me. These young fellows seem to understand men better.

Then he turned to describe the experience with new safety policies and their enforcement:

. . . But this [general foreman] — before he came here [some years before] they got men killed on the hot lines. They had men up there not qualified to do the work. Men were pretty scarce then and they didn't have any rubber goods. The general foreman has never had an accident . . .

He sums up,

We've got better equipment, better trucks. We got hole diggers now, heavy pole setting equipment. Now we've got hot sticks [to handle high-tension lines] . . . I think they're doing pretty good.

The psychological contract for "just a job" had turned out to be a lifetime arrangement, each segment of which fit well the needs of the individual man. Each change provided him with a better job than the one he had before, better in the sense that up to a point his skill increased and beyond that point change was in keeping with personal preferences. There was no experienced loss with each change. Nothing was being taken away from him psychologically for each change was congruent with changes within himself, and demands on him were in keeping with what he could give.

The acceptability of the changing contract was enhanced particularly by what he interpreted to be growing affection and appropriate control. Not only did the new equipment make the job easier over the years, but psychologically it was something of a gift, something he could use and take pride in. The work was more demanding — larger poles — and more important. The new managers understood more and cared more about the men and the more rigid precautions said that a man's life was too valuable to be squandered accidentally.

Change, in this man's experience, consistently met his legitimate dependency needs and made for increasing flexibility in the balancing of psychological distance. As the driver saw it, the company was a reliable partner. It had kept a psychological contract through merger, depression, technological change, and personal obsolescence. Each change increased the range of gratifications and helped him define more accurately what he could and could not do. Now, looking back as he neared retirement, he would observe in all honesty, "I couldn't see anything they could change . . ."

Contexts of Change

We noted in chapter I that there were three different perspectives on the past and future, depending on one's place and experience in the company. Whether any given change was important to a person and how he reacted to this change was significantly related to these perspectives.

These differing views of past and future help us to specify those areas of the psychological contract which are most sensitive to possible violation as the organization's needs change, and with them its expectations.

For example, the achievements of the company represented a definition of occupational identity for top level executives. They had "arrived." Their psychological contracts in a large measure had been fulfilled. Now their task was to maintain autonomy for the company and with it identity for themselves. Thus, to them, the threat of government-owned utilities and the strictures of regulatory bodies would always have personal, psychological as well as economic meaning. By way of contrast, the social disruptions which automation might cause would affect them very little.

As a result of merger, the functions of the higher level executives often changed so that they could not continue to provide support for middle management. Instead of being concerned with general administration over limited areas, top executives had to carry more specialized but company-wide responsibilities. There were now headquarters administrative specialists with whom middle management had to work. This change had little effect on top management, but it was critically important to middle management.

The individual occupational identities of top management could be said to be considerably more clearly defined than those of middle management. By definition, top management had "arrived."

Middle management in some ways had not. Those in top ranks made the major decisions and set the company-wide policies. Those in middle management who might move up would have to expand their perspective on the organization from the narrower area in which they had been working to company-wide problems. Despite whatever definition of occupational identity they had achieved, some change would be required in any upward move. Necessarily, then, middle management perceived its destiny as tied to the philosophy and decisions of top management.

It is not surprising that middle management should wish for a close affiliation with the power figures on whom it must depend. The mergers, as we understood their effects, by supplanting many personal relationships with formal procedures, increased the need to intensify those relationships which were left. But organizational needs for greater efficiency and lower costs resulted in still fewer personal relationships, thus violating the psychological contract.

Because the field groups would more readily define their occupational roles in terms of their specific skills and seniority, and because they were geographically closer to their own superiors, with lower levels of occupational aspiration, they did not yearn in the same degree for ties with top management. For many, only dimly aware of who the company's leaders were, the company itself, whatever that vague entity was, was the other partner in the contract and its major commitment was security.

CHANGE AND STRESS

Change is a fact of life. Every man must cope in some fashion with the inevitability of change, both in his personal life circumstances and in the organization in which he works. In the course of his working life, he moves from the status of neophyte to veteran. He may be promoted or transferred, sustain an injury, learn new skills or give up old ones. Meanwhile the company will be changing in various ways. The very name of the company may change in a merger. Policies change. Supervisors, peers, and subordinates come and go. The initial psychological contract is sub-

ject to significant change over the period of the relationship between man and organization. Neither knows what he will want
ultimately. Changing personnel, economic and political circumstances may well force either party to make demands on the other
different from those originally made.

The fact of change is not new, nor do we add anything by indicating that some people react to change in the company with
distress. When we examine change experiences, we see that only
those changes which are interpreted as violations of the psychological contract result in anger, withdrawal, hostility, and similar
reflections of distress.

The fact that some changes in the psychological contract do
not arise out of the changing expectancies of *both* parties does
not of itself constitute a violation of the psychological contract.
Violation occurs when the changing expectancies of one party are
imposed on and threaten the state of interdependence and the
balance in psychological distance achieved by the other.

In this chapter we have been discussing the changing expectancies of the company and their effects on these two processes.
If a group of employees decided not to come to work regularly
and refused to obey superiors while at the same time demanding
a reduction in hours of work, then they would have violated the
psychological contract by making it difficult for the company to
depend on them, by failing to maintain an appropriate psychological distance between themselves and their bosses, and by demanding that the company make an adaptation which it could
not make under those circumstances. Such a violation of the psychological contract would be as difficult for the company to cope
with as it is in reverse.

If change is not imposed, if it involves no loss of interdependence or psychological distance, or if it is not accompanied by increasing demand, then it appears not to be interpreted as a contractual violation. The partnership remains equally acceptable to
both parties.

Put another way, if interdependence and balanced distance can be maintained in the face of change, then the person has greater flexibility for coping with the stress of the increasing demands. Flexibility under stress means essentially the capacity to find adequate substitutes for that which has been lost or to make extraordinary efforts to meet demands.

In those examples in which organizational change and personal change were in the same direction, so that interdependence and balanced distance were not threatened, the men were able to find new sources of gratification (the Heirs) or retain continuing sources of gratification (the second group of Elders). Similarly, they were able to maintain a realistic view of their assets and limitations, or tolerate an altered view of their assets and limitations brought about by a change in life circumstances.

CHAPTER VII

THE OTHER SIXTEEN HOURS

Our study of Midland was focused primarily upon work life within the company. We have reported thus far on the development of the initial expectations and anticipations which employees and company brought to their relationship, and the transformation of these expectations into a psychological contract. We have examined the central concerns which people expressed — interdependence, balanced distance, and change — and have pointed up the ways in which efforts to deal with these concerns appear to be related to aspects of behavior characteristic of mental health.

In this exposition we have said little about home and community relationships. These, too, inevitably become intertwined with work life. Our understanding of the mental health aspects of work cannot be rounded out without some consideration of how work experience affects and is related to other aspects of living. Furthermore, our observations indicate that work, because of its importance for the total life adjustment of the person, has significant effects on his experience outside of work. Work can significantly influence the range and variety of sources of gratification to be found after working hours.

Shift Work

The work setting and the immediate situation of the job had direct influences on the gratifications which could be obtained in social-family life and the degree of work-home interaction. Shift work is a good example, for its effects invariably were described by those who worked on shifts.

In one of the power plants, difficulties connected with shift work were mentioned by eight of the ten men interviewed. One of the two men who did not comment was single and had no family responsibilities; the other had only recently come to work.

The men themselves had arranged their own shift work schedule in order to keep the plant in operation twenty-four hours a day. The arrangement in this plant called for shift changes every two weeks (other rotation patterns were followed at other plants). All of the men on one shift made the shift change together.

Each member of the group recognized how shift work impinged on him personally. He knew also that all the other men felt the same way. Each man seemed to accept the shift as a feature of work life, but one which exacted a heavy price from him. A junior foreman commented:

> Sometimes at eleven o'clock at night I feel sorry for myself. If you work shift work, you don't have any friends. They don't know whether you are sleeping or working . . . it's darn difficult during shift work. The school PTA meets and stuff like that that goes on in the evening and I am handicapped and can't go. You have an invite out and find you are working on the evening shift and you can't go . . . My wife, bless her heart, she is pretty good natured about that. It has hurt me. I like to get out once in awhile and visit. With small children, and you asleep in the daytime, that gets pretty rough at times.

A number of the men commented that the most difficult feature of shift work was the impossibility of establishing a regular eating and sleeping schedule. Almost as difficult to solve were the problems which shift work created when it came to engaging in community activities or special projects with the family. One operator noted, "I get grouchy after I have worked graveyards." Another operator said:

> With the shift work here it is pretty rough. You go home days and try to sleep; people will call up and beat on the doors, and maybe it is hot. Most of the fellows have air conditioners and that has relieved the problem of sleeping in hot weather. The guys working on lower salaries can't afford one, maybe . . . this would be an ideal job ex-

cept for the midnight to eight shift. You get on days and it's all gone. I guess we are just not made to act like hoot owls. I am not alone in this, all the fellows — it affects them the same. Shift work is very hard on the family. It is difficult for a wife. I have no friends other than the boys I work with. They are like me—they can't go out on Saturday night and get loaded if they want to because they have to go to work the next day. Once every six weeks I have a Saturday night I can go out on.

The foreman on this crew noted that,

We got a lot of boys here on mechanical and electrical maintenance who were operators — they got off because of that shift. It was their main complaint.

Shift work, destroying schedules and routines as it did, added psychological burdens for many of these men. Their guilt was increased because they knew that they should be participating more in activities involving their families, and because they badly needed the friends they felt they were losing in this way.

On the other hand, for the person who preferred to be somewhat isolated from others, shift work relieved him of community and family responsibilities to some degree. It was socially acceptable to claim exemption from home and community duties because of the nature of one's work, just as at work it was possible to avoid interaction with others because of the realistic demands of those jobs which required isolated work and attention to mechanical details.

Institutional Relationships

There was also a carry-over from the work organization to the other institutions in the community. People spontaneously described such things as the availability of bank credit on the basis of their work in the company. For example, a division superintendent in one of the larger cities described how the company's reputation was closely tied to the way in which individuals in the organization were viewed favorably by people in the community:

Every place I've been around the company, I have felt that working for Midland gives you first consideration with the merchants in and around town. It's a good job to have, especially for credit rating. Here . . . I get credit rating calls once in a while but all they ask is if I have so-and-so working for me, and whether he's been working steadily. If I tell them yes to that, that's all they seem to want to know . . . I had an experience in another town which brought home to me how people think about the company. A friend of mine in the Kiwanis Club said a foreman for the company lived next door to him and he thought it was real fine how he always went out in the storms . . . at night . . . I said to the man, "Of course, you know he's getting paid for all that extra time when the storms come along." The man said, "No, I didn't know that — but if he was being paid extra, he *should* be," but it still surprised him and pleased him very much that the company went all out to give such good service in bad weather . . .

These examples illustrate the manner in which the person's organizational identity became a basis for other relationships. Expectations about the other person are strongly determined by his work associations. "This is a good company to work for" frequently means that "other people respect me" or "other people envy me" because the company is seen to have "good standing" in the community.

Community Activities

Many of the managerial personnel spent much of their non-work time on civic activities. They carried their organizational identity as company representatives into their community interactions. The press toward community activity was a natural consequence of the business in which they found themselves and of their status.

This type of immersion in the community, characterized by a service orientation which seemed to go well beyond specific job demands, though more typical of managerial personnel, was certainly not limited to them. We can take as an example an outside districtman who functioned independently most of the time, meeting the service needs of several small communities some distance from the central office out of which he worked. He described his own job as follows:

> I handle everything from customer complaints to hot sticking [working with high-tension lines], collections, service, meter work, everything like that.

The way in which he saw his relationship to others in the community showed the considerable investment in these relationships which were an important part of the job to him and which extended beyond usual working hours.

> You've got to listen to people with sympathy and try to explain things to them. Some just don't have the patience to do that. After all, I think the individual wants a lot of attention. I don't care how small his complaint is, I try to give it as much time as I have to. For that matter, it's a little more time than usually is needed for those small things.

These examples indicate that one's work role can carry over considerably past the usual concept of the job as being "from eight to five." Company personnel were seen by neighbors and family as experts in a very important area of service. Considerable gratification was often associated with having one's role provide a basis for relationships to others in the community, not only during work but after work as well.

Outside Work

In addition to the carry-over of the job role into family and neighborhood, for a number of men the job led to other jobs. Often this extra work was an extension of what they did in the company. A particular job in the company made it possible to find extra work of the same type. Two illustrations indicate the close ties between the individual and the organization, economically and psychologically, and particularly the way in which the work role strongly influenced all of the activities of these men outside of their usual eight-hour working day.

A division auditor had been with the company for more than ten years at the time of the interview. He had not had extensive training in accounting but the experience which he had built up prior to joining the company and since had provided him with skills which he carried into off-the-job, income-producing activities. He kept books for several small business firms.

A division superintendent told how he had worked hard to get ahead during the years and slowly learned more skills. His long association with the company and the skills he learned not only provided him with security on the job but enabled him to set up his own business as well. His job with the company also provided the contacts for extra work off the job which brought him important additional income. He described the way in which his private interests and company interests fit together:

> I maintain a welder of my own . . . I could still eat with that thing [if the job fell through] . . . Then I lay plastic pipe to these irrigation wells. I do that week ends. The company sells them the gas, I sell them the pipe and lay it.

The Issue of Centrality

The findings of Robert Dubin (8), and Daniel Bell (5), concentrating on the bureaucratic and depersonalizing aspects of many work settings in our increasingly automated and complex industrial society, lead to the interpretation that the functions served by work and home are relatively distinct. These sociologists, from observations in mass production, urban situations, assert repeatedly that the deepest psychological investments and most significant experiences necessarily take place in life spheres other than work. Our experience at Midland would lead us to qualify such interpretations.

Continuities Between Work and Home

People at Midland whether working on the line, in the office, or in a plant, were for the most part both physically and psychologically "close" to life at home and in the community even while at work. The company's products and services, for one thing, were among the most important and familiar features of every household. Much of the daily routine consisted of services rendered directly to residential customers, who were at the same time often one's friends and neighbors. This experience was usual for the electric or gas crewman, who by his own efforts strung wires or laid pipe to the doors of local farmhouses or city dwellings. It was also the usual experience of women in the office, arranging for installation or termination of utility service and collecting money for services rendered, in direct contact with householder-customers.

Working at Midland offered stability, close and continuous relationships with other people on the job, and, generally speaking, a permissive work setting in which a man and woman could work in his or her own way to accomplish the necessary organizational tasks. These rather permissive and "homelike" characteristics of the company could be seen in many phases of its operations. For example, many employees, particularly at lower levels in the organization, were recruited through friendships with company people. At the same level, seniority weighed heavily along with technical qualifications and merit in consideration for promotion. Similarly, while work at these levels was typically planned and carried out according to an established routine, there was plenty of room for individual style in accomplishing the work. People were often able to work at a self-determined pace, following a sequence of activities they decided upon themselves and under the direction of supervisors who were helpful and supportive rather than authoritarian and impersonal.

Of course, people in various parts of the company organization often reported work experiences which were exceptions to this "homelike" picture. In the power plants, for example, where shift work was the rule and work routines were highly structured because of the nature of the operation, there was a sharper psychological separation of work and home. Some jobs — gas transmission, the work of the traveling auditor, and emergency work of all kinds — broke the continuity between work and home for many people in the company. For the middle manager, civic activities which amounted to a necessary part of his job often took hours from time at home over and above his normal time in the office. But such discontinuities were the exception rather than the rule at Midland.

Complementarity

People at Midland frequently spoke about the way in which work and home experiences could *complement* one another.

A power plant maintenance man saw a healthy and rewarding continuity between life on and off the job. He told of the importance of dealing with other crew members as individuals, since what went on at home could affect what happened on the job. He said that when a man had outside interests and enjoyed working on community projects, the day's work seemed to go more smoothly. He himself had spent many years in roving assignments in the construction industry, so he had gained special satisfaction from the type of activities off the job which working in the plant made possible:

I like this job here because I'm home every night except when I'm on call — that doesn't happen very often. Perhaps twice a month all through the year. It gives me time for some other things. Like club work. I'm in the Optimist Club here, active in local government. I guess I've got too many jobs. Money is not coming in as fast [as in construction] but when you are located in one place that doesn't matter . . . In construction work you make good money but you really have to maintain two homes. You work on a job like that, you're not affiliated with any clubs, but you know every bar in town. A person should weigh the advantages of the job not just for the money but for what it would be for the family.

A similar kind of complementarity was reported by the clerk in a company office located in her home town. She believed that some days "work takes a lot out of you" but went on to tell how her experiences at work broadened her horizons, and how this broadening in turn made more pleasurable the essentially quiet and simple life she led when not at work:

> This has always been my home. I've known most of the people. On trying days work probably affects home life when I get home tired. But it doesn't happen any more here than it would in any other job. It's brought me in contact with people that I otherwise wouldn't have met. I am a member of the Business and Professional Woman's Club here and we exchange ideas and tell about our jobs . . .

In a number of company locations, this gratifying type of congruence between experiences at work and at home was reported not only by isolated individuals but also by most of the members of a working group. In a small power plant, a number of workers in both the operating and maintenance forces spoke of their community activities, which ranged from Boy Scout leadership to home-building. These activities were pursued both with community friends and with work associates. And the gratification experienced from their outside activities was often among the reasons for liking the job. People valued the fact that in many cases work associations extended into other life spheres. In a sense, such groups consciously encouraged the fusion of home and work.

In cases such as these, there was psychological investment in both life spheres, investment in one tightly bound to investment in the other. It was evident here that whatever gratifications were available to the person at work were enhanced because of the part work played in the total life of the community in which the person lived and spent his time after leaving the job. Thus the congruence of work and home life widened the range of potential gratifications in the experience of many Midland people.

It will be recalled from chapter V that some parts of the company were considerably isolated from others. The close physical proximity of work and family living and the isolation of both in small communities made for a number of special problems. When work and home experiences could not be adequately separated, some of the gratifications which might have been possible in either area were lost to both. There was an attempt to avoid these difficulties by carefully regulating the interaction between individuals and groups off the job. Although there can be a complementary relationship between work and home, the two areas must be sufficiently distinct from each other that one can complement the other. If the two spheres are essentially one, no complement is possible.

Compensation

There was frequent evidence, too, of how home life could compensate for the lack of certain sources of gratification at work. This was particularly true in the case of an apprentice lineman. As a green youngster, he was highly frustrated to observe the skill of his elders, a skill which he felt he could never attain nor, he thought, would work ever have the same meaning for him as it did for them. He could not see himself becoming as dedicated to his work as they were. He was further unhappy because of the low status of his position and the number of years which he would have to wait to have higher status. His description of what he did on his time off reflected how he used this time to satisfy his needs for independence and excitement which he could not at that point satisfy on the job. He said:

I like to go home and clean up — take a good hot shower — then I hop on my cycle and take off just to cruise around town and [chuckling] look for women. Of course, I don't have to look very far 'cause I'm acquainted with a number of young ladies around town . . . then I like to tinker with the cycle. I like to drag out my own .22 and go out and find a squirrel. Sunday afternoon I usually go over to ——— to the stock car races. The other day they had a [motorcycle] competition out at ——— . . .

Either work or home alone may not serve adequately to meet a person's needs and favored modes of maintaining his psychological equilibrium. Particular frustrations experienced in one sphere can frequently be compensated for by balancing satisfactions in the other sphere. The result over a period of time can represent rather satisfactory psychological equilibrium for the individual. Marital status, age, and particularly personality configurations necessarily play a part in those aspects of work and home which are more or less satisfying to people.

A bookkeeper in a small office described her working world. She said she went to work because she needed money, but quickly she qualified her statement:

I also have three children who get on my nerves, as much as I love them.

She said that this was her first full-time job since she married. She added that her job "also helped her handle her feelings about the children." She was active in church affairs and in P.T.A. She offered as her main reason for enjoying the social activities and her occupational activities the opportunity of being with other women. Doing housework repeatedly did not appeal to her.

She continued to talk about her work, saying that the most important factor about her work as far as she was concerned was "the sense of accomplishment that I get when the accounts balance." The interviewer asked her to describe her feelings in greater detail. She replied,

Let me see how I can tell you about it. Yes, it is a very special feeling. I get a kick out of it, like when my babies were born.

There are things that I don't know as well as I should. In fact, for some time I was scared I would not be able to handle the job left by the other girl. [after a pause] One reason I like to go out is that my husband doesn't like to go and I do. In fact, he takes care of the children at home . . . maybe the reason is that I was kind of lonesome. I just got to feel pretty lonely at home until I got my job. Now I feel less lonely.

After describing something of her office work and the people who worked with her, she added,

. . . I think there are a lot of women who feel lonely. Well, yes, I know this from talking with quite a few. I've found that my housework is lighter and more pleasant since I work. It is now a different routine and also I have bought things that have made work lighter at home.

Had the supervisors who employed this woman and others like her asked them why they wanted to work, probably they would have said for additional family income. Presumably they wanted "just a job." But their part of the original psychological contract was something else. They wanted to escape from loneliness, from what they regarded as intolerable home conditions or from their children. Though in one sense they wanted little from the company (advancement, vocational skills) in the form of initial expectations, in another sense they came with intense expectations that in work they would find relief from some of the psychological burdens they carried.

And they did. Although the experience of change, even to a psychologically rewarding job, was not easy, the job began to make it possible to maintain a more comfortable distance from both children and home chores. Through the initial months of fear, doubt, and anxiety, they began to establish ties to their work. There was, in addition, a new source of gratifying dependent needs. There were other women, and a work structure with job demands. The company required something of them, and paid them for it. There was a sense of completion, complementing that of being a mother and wife, and a sense of value because someone in return for their work gave them an amount of money, a highly important symbol of value in Western society.

Work made it possible to expand the variety of sources of gratification, but at the same time it did not alienate them from the home or their families. Certainly they were somewhat uneasy leaving their children, in a culture which still believed that a mother's place was in the home. But in work they were able to compensate for the psychological deprivations at home, to displace their anger onto constructive job effort, and to extend their personal breadth. As a result, they were, according to their report, more efficient in their homemaking tasks, and easier to live with.

Displacement

Displacement from one of these life spheres to the other was reported often. Numerous examples illustrated the ways in which home problems were brought to work and vice versa.

A crane operator in one power plant, speaking of some of the positive and negative aspects of his work, made this observation, echoed by others:

> Say a man comes to work and he's got some problems at home — at times maybe he's not thinking about what he is doing or if he has some difficulty out here, he might go home and say something mean to a member of the family . . . possibly there are men out here with family problems on their mind — or work — they are hard to get along with.

Except in rare cases, usually those in which denial of any angry feelings was obvious, people mentioned the potentiality for displacing angry feelings and reactions from one sphere to the other. At times they reported experiences of being ignored by co-workers, or themselves ignoring spouses after getting home. Often expressions of anger were reported at other times. People spoke of finding themselves being short-tempered with their children and realizing in the midst of an outburst that they were being difficult to live with because of something unpleasant during the day.

Flight from Both Work and Home

Some, of course, could not use either work or home in complementary ways. For them both home and work life seemed to create obligations and burdens which would have been unbearable were it not for the opportunities they created to "get away from it all" in essentially solitary activities.

A line foreman told of the tensions he lived with in his daily work which stemmed from physical danger to the crew, the role conflict which he experienced as both member of management and member of the crew, and the problems of being a leader.

He moved up to foreman by the seniority route and could not go "back to the hooks" (the lineman's equipment for climbing poles) because he was now too old and heavy. First he described the nature of his daily work as he experienced it:

You think about the boys' safety a lot. I go home just pooped. You worry about them. You feel like you would fly [away] if they slipped. It's just the normal reaction. It makes you feel as if you're still up there with them just as if you were on the pole. It makes me just as scared as they are when their feet slip. You got to be kind of go-between, too. You've got to play both sides. You've got to stay on the good sides of the boys and the company to keep both of them in good humor. The company sends orders down and you've got to work that out with the fellows. [As an example, he pointed to the safety helmet on his knees.] The thing there was a big incident [when the company required the men to wear the helmets]. The men were griped at me and at the company. I had my say to ———— [the safety man] but I didn't get nowhere. So I told the boys we had to go along with it, it looked like . . . they come out with some other orders the boys just can't see. Then it's up to me to make the thing stick.

Somewhat later in the interview, he described with quiet enthusiasm how much it meant to him to "get away from it all." When asked what he liked to do in his off-time, he said,

Fish. I got a little cabin on the lake. I like to go up there on the week end and get some grub and build a fire. The gate is locked and no one else can get in except those that have cabins there. Mama and the girls come out on Sunday and bring my dinner. My wife would sit out there for days if she could. She's trying to get me to take up bowling and golf, but I don't go for any of that. I don't like to hunt. I just like it out there at the little cabin . . . I like to get out alone there. That's the good life.

A somewhat similar experience was reported by an engineer in another town. Here, there was no acknowledgment by the man himself that life at work lacked satisfaction for him. However, from both peers and supervisors came numerous comments that the man was overwhelmed by his job, could not plan the work or make decisions, and had been responding to increasing pressure for higher production by using more and more sick leave.

He and his wife spent the evening hours by going to the movies every time the shows changed in the local theaters. In past years, it had been possible to escape from some of his problems by returning to work, not by going back to the warehouse, but by thinking alone at home about work problems. Now he could no longer do this either. He said it was more comfortable simply to get out of the house.

Both of these men were unable to compensate for home in work or vice versa, and therefore had to flee from both scenes.

The Individual's Responsibility

Some have contended that "ninety percent of all emotional disturbances on the job come from home." Others have argued that industry should have no interest in problems of mental health because most such problems have to do with family relationships. Both of these arguments deny the essential psychological importance of work and the inevitable psychological relationship between a man's work experience and the rest of his life.

To decry this extreme position is not to take the other extreme. Not all of the influences on mental health are to be found at work, nor can any management possibly counteract all of those forces which may limit those behaviors indicative of mental health. The power plants at Midland, for example, had to operate 24 hours a day. Someone had to work each of those hours. The men themselves chose their shift arrangement as the best compromise which could be made, even though some of their gratifications were limited. Similarly, not all of the talents and assets of each person can be put to maximum use in any business organization, and many tasks must be done regardless of whether they meet people's needs.

Part of the contribution of work experience to mental health lies in what goes on on the job, part in what a relationship to an organization makes possible for people in that part of their lives away from work. And many of the constructive influences for mental health must be found outside of work. The experiences we have described in this chapter indicate that people themselves take a large share of the responsibility for making best use of the resources for mental health which only they can draw from both spheres.

CHAPTER VIII

RECIPROCATION

ONE afternoon a researcher and a general foreman were riding in the latter's truck outside of town. There were large black thunder clouds in the west. At 5:30 p.m., the storm hit. The rain came down in sheets — so hard that the windshield wipers could not keep up and the truck slowed down to a crawl. Calls began to come from the general foreman's office on the two-way radio. The researcher made this chronology of succeeding events as they occurred:

5:35: A call comes that a transformer has blown on the south side of town.

5:45: A line is down on Sussex Street and a hot wire is in the alley. The general foreman and researcher go to check it.

5:45: General foreman calls in for a crew to cut the switch on the line which is hot so that it can be put up again.

5:50: General foreman and researcher return to warehouse. A substation reports it has no power. The superintendent is in the warehouse office. A line foreman comes in. A service truck goes out to open the switches on the 100 block of Sullivan. A radio station reports a tornado on the ground west of town.

6:05: A second truck leaves to repair lines in the south part of town. The general foreman has taken over the radio and telephones in the office. The superintendent sits down in a chair beside the general foreman's desk . . . The general foreman talks on the radio, does all the dispatching. The superintendent sits by.

6:10: A highway patrolman reports a funnel sighted five miles south of his position. The radio station reports the funnel heading for the town.

6:15: The town siren sounds. The superintendent suggests that managers in outlying communities should be alerted. He places a call to them. Another report comes in that a 12-kv line south of town to the rural customers is out of service.

6:20: The highway patrol reports three funnels on the ground. A service call is coming in about every thirty seconds. The superintendent asks the general foreman if the lines south of town can be sectionalized and the general foreman says no, that you wouldn't do that anyway unless the wires were actually down . . .

6:25: More calls from a rural area south of town.

6:30: The general foreman wants to look at a rural line which is out. Two more men come in and the superintendent asks the general foreman how he wants to use them.

6:31: Report of a funnel four miles south of town. At the same time a call comes from a truck on the 100 block of Sullivan that the lines are now clear and they are ready to close the switch. The superintendent tells them to hold off for another order from the general foreman on this.

6:32: The superintendent calls the sheriff's office to tell them that a line is down on the rural road that people should watch out because the line is hot. The sheriff says they will cover.

6:45: A number of calls indicate that most of the rural lines south of town are out.

6:55: More men come in. The general foreman is on the radio and not free to talk. Another funnel cloud a hundred feet off the ground is reported moving northeast in the central part of the state.

6:56: Researcher and general foreman leave to check a rural line and they pick up the manager.

7:15: They arrive at the rural area, finding only slight damage. There is another report from a radio station that a funnel is on the ground headed directly for town. However the storm seems to be abating.

7:25: Crews are all pulled back into town.

7:30: General foreman, researcher, and manager are in the truck. The general foreman hears on the radio the superintendent giving a switching order, and he corrects the order from the radio of his truck. The manager comments: "It's a damn good thing you're sitting here to figure that one out." The general foreman answers, "I'm scared on this switching when he gets to doing that — either he'll burn something up or someone will get killed." He says that the superintendent thought there were outages but actually there was only one out and the others were caused because the switch was open.

7:40: The manager is dropped off at his house.

7:45: They stop at a gas station and then head for the office. More outages are reported south of town. When the researcher and general foreman get back to the office, the superintendent is still operating the radio. The general foreman mutters, "He's moved in and now I can't operate — you notice that." Another man is in the office now helping with the phone calls.

8:00: A local manager calls in that all is calm in his town. There are more heavy storm clouds and lightning in the west.

8:10: All districts report they are operating again. The general foreman sends a crew to eat. The superintendent goes out to look at the storeroom — he is the only one with a key to it.

8:25: Another report from radio stations that a tornado has been sighted 30 miles west. Others are reported south.

8:45: The general foreman gets back on the radio and clears up the remaining service calls on his desk.

8:55: Another report of a tornado on the ground.

8:55: Gas station man comes over to say he has some gas in cans in case the pump near the office goes out.

9:20: The general foreman and researcher go to eat.

In these four hours of coping with an emergency, many men left the safety and comfort of their homes, ready to "pitch in." Some worked with others who were not their regular work partners. There was not time for extensive planning of work, and discussion of what might be done was at a minimum. The men were called upon to coordinate their work under extremely dangerous circumstances. Despite the multiple demands on the crews, power was restored in a relatively short time.

In addition to having to meet the extraordinary demands of the emergency, the men were confronted with stress resulting from the behavior of the superintendent. At times the superintendent took over the general foreman's job. He did so in a way that demonstrated to all of the men that he was making decisions beyond his knowledge. This loss of psychological distance might well have undermined the interdependence of the crews and the general foreman, and that of the general foreman and the superintendent. "He moved in and now I can't operate," said the general foreman. The men could not help but know of a conflict between the two superiors which might threaten interdependence even further, for according to the psychological contract they would expect consistent and supportive guidance. They could not get much guidance from clashing superiors who gave conflicting directions. They would have difficulty identifying themselves with a superior whose power was being vitiated. In the face of temporary but severely increased task demands, the men were threatened with some psychological loss.

How, then, do we account for the fact that the men were able to do their job so efficiently? In the emergency, the general foreman clearly took charge. He checked the trouble spots first hand. The men depended on the general foreman and he on them; both of them were aware of that fact despite the superintendent's behavior. Even in the emergency the general foreman maintained an appropriate distance from them. Though he gave directions and personally inspected the scene, he did not interfere in the steps of the work which the men had to do, leaving them to function independently. He exercised control without invading privacy. Even though he was angry with the superintendent, his central focus remained on the task. At the same time, by seeing to it that the men had their meal, he demonstrated his interest in and concern for them. The dependence of the organization on the men was clear in its need for them to restore service.

In short, efforts were being made to fulfill the psychological contract despite the pressures of the situation. We may infer from that fact that a reasonably consistent effort to fulfill the contract was characteristic of previous operations in this unit. There was a history of relationships between the men and the company characterized by interdependence, balanced distance, and mutual coping with change. The interaction of these processes, the total process of fulfilling the psychological contract, we call reciprocation.

We infer that because reciprocation had functioned reasonably well before, the strength of the relationship between the men and the company was such that they were able to be flexible under stress and therefore to cope successfully with the emergency.

In the preceding chapters we discussed the elements of reciprocation separately. We examined some of the expectations of employees and company which together came to comprise a psychological contract. We considered reciprocal aspects of the central concerns discussed by Midland people: interdependence, balanced distance and mutual coping with change. We noted some of the relationships between work experience and life outside of work. Throughout our discussion we traced the evolution of various components of the psychological contract which enabled us to view work experience in an organization as an effort to fulfill certain psychological needs on the part of people and organizational needs on the part of the company. In this example, in four hours of crises, we saw the whole intertwined process in microcosm.

Let us now examine reciprocation more closely. We cannot at this point purport to examine it completely because there are, no doubt, other components of the process of which we are not yet aware. We can, however, try to understand those parts of the process we have come to know. Our vehicle for this examination is the self-description of a manager. To understand the first part of his story, the reader should know that in the early days of electricity, many municipalities established their own electric generating and distributing systems. As independent units, these often were not economical. Private utilities bought many of these independent units and integrated them into larger systems. This is what is meant by the phrase "buying up towns."

The manager spent most of his work life at Midland. He took a steady utility job after high school and, upon the recommendation of a friend, came to Midland. He spoke of the broad experience he began to gain early:

The man who was "buying up towns" took me under his wing . . . it was an education for me to see how he worked with them [the small town councils]. Then a problem came up. As he would buy these towns and absorb them, they would be off by themselves. They weren't tied together in any way. I saw an opportunity for someone to manage those towns — I went to see Mr. ———— about that and told him I thought someone was needed to put that together . . . I did everything. I collected bills, was stand-by engineer at the little plant, sold ice out of the ice house. I did everything except climb poles . . . I was interested in making our division more respectable, in growing. You want to build yourself all the time, of course. Well, they gave me (other) towns . . . One pleasant thing about this job is helping these young fellows come along . . . they might just as well benefit from my years of experience . . .

As he looked back on his career, he said:

I don't know of anything else I'd rather do — in fact I can talk to [the chairman of the board and the president] very easily.

It's fine to know when I'm sick that my pay check will continue to come in and that my affairs will all be handled — what if I were running a filling station, or my own grocery store, how could I come back and move sacks of potatoes around and stuff like that? I would have been wiped out . . . In spite of [illness] I got my raise each year . . . It would have taken all the starch out of me if they had kept my salary the same or cut back a little bit.

I look at it like this. An organization like this has been the means of me coming out of high school . . . and with the opportunities they gave me I was able to develop a place for myself — to get pleasure out of my work, to prosper within reason, and feel confident that you're doing something for those people in Shaw, the people here in Kena, and the people here in the office.

The manager began to work for a utility when he was in high school. His early entrance into the company from another utility already indicated some definition of occupational identity. He came with the idea "you want to build yourself," and that an organization "like this" would enable him to develop a place for himself through which he could make his life's contributions. He expected the company to make it possible for him to fulfill certain of his needs and goals. He wanted to depend on the company; he expected the company to depend on him. There was, in fact, interdependence.

From the beginning of his experience in the company, there were people who guided him, encouraged him, and stood by him. By encouraging and instructing him, a superior showed his interest, gave support and added to the new man's self-esteem, rewards which enhanced identification with the superior. The novice acquired specific skills, "It was an education for me," which he then was given an opportunity to apply. He was now in some ways different than he had been before. He saw opportunities to manage and to deal with problems which expanded his skills.

As he built himself, he built the company and, in some measure, the community. He defined a role as manager, he expanded that role and was recognized by others in that role. He taught others how to do his job as he had learned to do it. He was apparently able to obtain reasonably balanced personal relationships with his associates. The behavior of higher officials toward him not only made him feel worthy, but also stirred him to help others. When illness struck, company officials went out of their way to help him. The personal support which he was given enabled him to cope more effectively with this drastic change in his life. He, in turn, supported new men and dedicated himself to the service of his three publics: the customers, the employees, and his superiors.

The manager's job was not without its problems. He described one of the crisis situations he had faced, a franchise fight. An election was held to decide if the company's franchise would be renewed:

> It was a very trying time. I tried to do right by all these people [in the community] and it was very disappointing to me to see so many led by this false stuff — false advice and information and just lies . . . Something like that is bad for a town — people take sides and they don't like to back up once they have their opinions made — they almost became enemies in some cases.

As he described in detail fighting the opposition, the gathering of petitions, and difficulties with political figures in the community, it was easy to see that here was Mr. Utility Company who was the focus of attack, and who, in his community and in his own eyes, could never escape being Mr. Utility. Man and company together were threatened, and together fought back. When man and company confront threat together, they are forced into the closest possible relationship. We would suggest that people who have such experiences are reluctant to think of leaving a company, even putting aside the question of age and retirement.

Noteworthy in this man's story, too, was the absence of compulsion. Except for the operation of reciprocation, there was no requirement that he remain in the company.

For neither party, however, was the psychological contract clear in the beginning. Neither the manager nor the representative of the company who hired him knew what might come of their relationship. As the manager initiated an action on behalf of the company and himself, the company responded, or the company initiated and the man responded. With each action and its complement, the contract changed. Neither the manager nor his superiors experienced imposition by the other or a feeling of loss in these changes. The manager assumed greater responsibilities; the company put more of itself in the hands of the man, even to the point of having him shape a part of it.

Reciprocation facilitated the refinement of his identity, and that of the company. The manager incorporated an idealized image of the company. To others, he became the company personified and personalized. It was almost as if company and man were interchangeable, as if one were or could be the other at times. Reciprocation is evident in behavior of both parties, a psychological bonding process, tying one to the other.

The manager said he knew no other job he would rather do and that the purposes and ideals of the organization were also his. Reciprocation had flowered.

Conditions for Reciprocation

From this example, and from our discussion in previous chapters, several organizational conditions appear to be necessary for reciprocation to develop with the person. Stated in the form of opportunities, these are:

1. to plan at least some part of one's work life; an area of freedom to function.

2. to model one's self upon authority figures in the company.

3. to act on the organization, to shape it to some extent to one's own values.

4. to experience oneself and the organization as confronting stress together.

5. to obtain the gratification of psychological needs for dependence and support.

6. to be controlled, or to have personal controls enhanced by the demands of the company.

7. to have the feeling of a fair-share partnership with the company.

8. to be stimulated, which includes the experience of growth and change.

These conditions appear to operate conjointly, all necessary for reciprocation to reach its fullest development. The eight conditions might be restated in many different ways. All could be related to interdependence alone. Most could also be related to balanced distance and the problems of coping with change.

The manager described some aspects of his own behavior which by our criteria would be mentally healthy. He mentioned a variety of sources of gratification through his relations with his company. He described ways he had successfully met stress situations, and activities in which he was able to meet some of the needs of the others. He recognized the limitations of his education but nonetheless, through the medium of the company, was able to make good use of his abilities with satisfying and productive results. This is not to say that this man is a paragon of mental health, or that his relations with his company made him mentally healthy. It is to say that reciprocation enabled him to fulfill many needs. His behavior in the course of the fulfillment could be described, according to our criteria, as mentally healthy. Put another way, reciprocation is a process of conflict resolution.

So far we have given several partial definitions of reciprocation. At this point let us summarize them. Reciprocation is the continuous process of fulfilling the psychological contract be-

tween employee and organization. In this process the employee
resolves conflict about interdependence, balanced distance, and
change as part of his effort to attain and maintain an adult occupational identity. As these conflicts are being resolved, their
resolution contributes to the solution of many of the company's
problems related to people and organizational objectives.

As a result of this process, an employee incorporates many of
the ideals, values, and purposes of the organization into his own
personality. He comes to feel that many of the company's interests are his personal interests as well. When reciprocation is operating well, the organization becomes personalized in the individual. He stands for all to see, as it were, that he and the company are in many respects as one. At the same time, the process
makes it possible for the organization to be changed in some degree by the employee, regardless of his place in the hierarchy,
and to adopt some of his values.

In short, reciprocation is a process which ties man and organization together for the accomplishment of their mutual tasks and
the resolution of their mutual conflicts.

Having considered the functioning of reciprocation, the conditions under which it operates, and the purposes it serves, three
important but parenthetical aspects should now be mentioned.
The first is the required precondition for reciprocation: investment by both parties. The second is a qualification about the direction of reciprocation. We have spoken so far as if reciprocation operated primarily through the mediation of superiors; it
operates as well in relationships to subordinates. Third, some recent studies on ego gratifications might seem to imply that reciprocation is not important to line-level people. Our observations
are quite the opposite.

Lack of Investment

By its very nature, reciprocation requires psychological investment by both parties. Though the company wields the greater

power in the relationship because it employs, assigns, directs, discharges the employee, the company cannot compel psychological investment from those who do not wish to invest. The company, in its own self-interest, will usually want to encourage reciprocation. But some employees will be unable to respond no matter what the organization does. Another middle management man is a case in point. Drawing an organization chart of his areas of responsibility, he said at the very beginning of his interview:

It's a screwball setup as far as I'm concerned. These guys here [drawing boxes for two] are over the line area, ———— is over our accounting. This is a kind of dual proposition the way I see it. They're supposed to be under me too. It seems to me everyone has authority but no one has responsibility.

He went on to enumerate people who acted as if they were his superiors but who technically were not. He noted that these people also gave orders directly to the line crews and the servicemen who were under him. Then he added,

But I have to be under these guys [referring to the group which he had just named], too. I don't get it.

He contrasted unfavorably his present mode of operation with a previous mode of operation under a different boss.

Let us look at the contract. This manager was part of a former company which had merged with Midland. He described the merger as "so they took over me and three old trucks." There was almost no initial investment and seemingly little expectation, just passive acceptance. He described transfer from one small community to another with little excitement or gratification, noting that he came to a manager's position almost by accident by virtue of having been around in a given area, over a period of time.

He found it difficult to establish reciprocation with the larger organization. He saw his former company toward which he still had positive feelings, as a smaller, intimate organization.

You didn't get so much kicking around if you wanted to know something.

His rosy view of the past might well have been a function of his inability to advance, a failure easily displaced onto the growing organization. Psychologically the past is nearly always overvalued and perceived in retrospect as more pleasant than the present. This is one way of dissipating the disappointment of not advancing for whatever reasons, but in this theme of alienation the personal meaning of the company to the man is apparent.

Having defined himself as of little value ("me and three old trucks"), the manager began his relationship with the merged company with a feeling of being at a loss. He kept putting himself in situations where the company's actions confirmed his conclusion. Almost every demand then was a stress for him.

His interview continued in a cynical vein: Other men were criticized for, in turn, criticizing employees who had done something wrong. Employees were criticized for using company equipment to earn money on their own over the week ends, a practice which he said had stopped. There were conflicts when he arranged for men to do jobs and then they were given contradictory orders by his supervisors. He said he took those up with his superiors and they replied that what he wanted done was less important to the over-all operation than that which they wanted done. He projected his own internal conflicts onto everyone in the company, blaming the problems which came to him on what he alleged to be conflict in the general office, about which he could have only very little first-hand knowledge.

I don't believe we have enough operating heads in the general office that understand the problem of the people outside. We'd have more concise and clear line of command with authority and responsibility better defined.

The complaints continued: the company didn't pay for his country club dues; the company didn't permit him to change girls around on the job when one was more fitted for the job than the other. Even the interviewer was met, as the interviewer felt it, with a "what's the use" attitude.

Here was the definition of his world by a man who essentially drifted, almost floating from one minor position to another, unable to invest himself and with little anticipation or expectation. He had not defined very clearly an occupational identity, despite his position. He had little self-esteem and limited support. Everyone above him was psychologically like a father giving orders, but, as he viewed it, none gave affection or cared. Interdependence was minimal, psychological distance from others too great, and he had no effective way of coping with change. Reciprocation seemed hardly to exist.

Though he represented the company, he was not the company and what was more he did not want to be the company. He continued a lifetime of marginal operations, getting by because he was in a small community. He projected all his problems onto everyone else. As he saw it everybody else was having friction.

A high degree of bypassing of this man occurred. Certainly the helpless, hopeless, unspirited feeling could lead only to the most tenuous of relationships between man and organization. Although he entered the company by merger, actually his expectation was closer to having joined it by chance. The company, he expected, would make something of him. Rather than being interdependent with the company, it might almost be said that he was exploiting the company for his own dependent needs.

The company kept him in his job. Though his superiors found it necessary to go around him they did not fire him because he did some things reasonably well and his unit met its basic obligations. Apart from some satisfaction of dependent needs, there was little pleasure in this man's work experiences. He was unable to see others in any but a critical way. He was all too aware of his limits, but found it hard to accept them. He was unable to deal with being constantly bypassed and reacted with repetitive grumbling, but made no effort at active resolution. He was not as productive as either he or the company would have wished.

Reciprocation in Subordinate Relationships

Although we have given most of our attention to relationships between people and their superiors, for those who have supervisory responsibilities, reciprocation includes subordinates and superiors. This is particularly true of general foremen, line foremen, and those in similar positions. The general foreman is concerned with his sensitivity to his men and with their needs. He is not without direct ties to higher management which, after all, has promoted him and holds him responsible for his functions. He talks much, however, about his men and his relationships with them. More than anyone else he must get the men to work. He must produce tangible results.

Certainly there are periods of physical stress such as described earlier in which a general foreman and his men must meet the crises of weather and emergency. Physical stress which is not so severe or prolonged as to become psychological stress does not seem to be experienced as something which man and organization confront together and therefore does not appear to facilitate reciprocation. It does not result in the same internal anxiety reported by the manager who had to endure a franchise fight. It does not have the same quality of anguish.

Conspicuously missing from the interview with the general foreman, to follow, and noticeably absent in other interviews with lower echelon people, is any mention of a specific person whose interest in the interviewee encouraged him or provided an identification figure.

The relationships of many middle management people like general foremen tend to lack two qualities which enhance reciprocation. Rarely do such people experience threat on behalf of or together with the company as did the first manager we described at the beginning of this chapter. In addition, these people tend to have fewer occupational identification figures.

Thus, though there are continuing elements of reciprocation, there is somewhat different emphasis for different levels in the organizational hierarchy.

A general foreman was interviewed in the warehouse. He began his electrical career going from a marginal farm to "pretty good money at that time . . . A man that goes into line work is a fellow that wants something different . . ." He came to Midland from another company. "Coming into an organization such as the power company you find you're in a bigger situation. It's more steady . . . There's more stuff to learn in the power company, the technical end. A man don't want to be a construction lineman all his life."

He reported that he had worked on a crew for several years under a foreman who suffered a severe illness. With his superiors's approval, he had done much of the foreman's work so the foreman would not have to give up his job. He said that he took his present job under the condition that he could be

boss of my men. I don't want no changes coming through affecting the crews that don't go through me first. They set it up that way and it's been that way . . . they want you to take the people and run the job as it ought to be run . . . I'm the type of guy that will speak up. If I see where I can save the company some money, that's what I do.

You've got to work along into people and get them to cooperate with you . . . you've got to let the men know you're a lineman. That you know a lineman's way of thinking and a lineman's working conditions. If they want a safety hook, it's your job to get it for them. And you don't pass the buck . . .

. . . the most important thing is the men. You gotta work with them and for them. You know and I know you can get a lot more out of people if you get at them the right way . . . If you criticize a man because he's not moving fast enough, it makes him sick and if he's the foreman all the people get sick on the crew. If you've got hazardous conditions, you want him to feel calm about it because you want him thinking about that job and not about some fracas he may be having with you.

The psychological contract in this case called for a range of experiences. He not only wanted more money, but also more opportunity.

He wanted to "be something" other than a construction lineman. Only later did management's side of the psychological contract change, although for him the expectation had been present from the first.

He observed early in his career that the company took care of its men, that it could be depended upon. Thus the model was established of the acceptability of helping others, recognizing them as individuals, and the safety of recognizing one's own limitations. The company would and did protect him.

The foreman could carry out the ideals of the company, which were also his, only if there were controlled relationships which bound both him and the company. He trusted that the company wanted him to "run things the way they should be run." They chose him for the job and that demonstrated high regard for him.

There were many gratifications from the job. The company told him in effect that his way of doing his job and the company's way were the same. There was no experience of loss or imposed demand; rather he and the company together would work out their joint problems.

The men regarded him as a parental figure. They tested him to see if they could depend upon him and identify themselves with him. Would he protect them from accidents? Would he get the tools they needed? "You gotta work with them and for them," he said. He saw himself as an agent of reciprocation for those to whom he was an authority figure.

The Question of Ego Satisfaction

The results of questionnaire studies have been interpreted to mean that line-level employees are not concerned with ego satisfactions at work. Gurin, Veroff, and Feld (14), for example, define the degree of ego satisfaction (personal involvement) in the job as "the extent to which an individual seeks some expression and actualization of the self in his work . . ." They then conclude, "It would appear . . . that most of these blue collar workers either come to the job situation with minimal ego-fulfillment aspirations or begin with aspirations but become adjusted to the lack of ego fulfillment on the job. In either case, the minimal opportunities for fulfillment are apparently not experienced by them as a lack or frustration, *at least at the conscious level* (italics ours)."

In our terms, this would mean that reciprocation would not function well at this level. Our experience at Midland indicated that the degree to which it functions varies among line-level people as it does among management people, depending in part on their investment and in part on what the company does. Let us take two examples, typical of many.

A gas compressor station engineer came from a farm family and was graduated from high school. Before working in the compressor station he had worked for a retail gas dealer. "This work had appealed to me before; I had always liked engines and gas service work." He liked his job because,

In the first place, it is a utility company and is always in demand, a continuous job. It is an insured job, although it doesn't pay enough or as much as other places.

After a pause he added,

I'm not sure about what other things are important. Well, the good pay, continuous job, and retirement benefits. I kinda feel bad when I'm not appreciated or listened to . . . but it doesn't happen here too often. When you have a job to do and you're not designated, just told, "I want you fellows to do this," it irritates me not to be clearly set what I am supposed to do.

He saw the future as possibly holding a promotion but,

There are some other jobs in this plant that I'd like to have, but the pay is the same . . . there are two ways of looking at it [leaving the company]. First of all, the money, then secondly the many years of security. After you're forty years old one would want many guarantees. It would be foolish to give this up although I'd very much like to move in the same company . . . I've been in one place all my life. I would like to move and acquire more friends.

Nothing in the interview provided a clear image of this man as an individual. Although he contracted for economic security, beneath his economic expectations lay an equally heavy expectation for emotional security. "I kinda feel bad when I'm not appreciated . . . it irritates me not to be clearly set what I am supposed to do." According to his expectations, an authority figure must give affection and direction.

The original psychological contract was limited — a steady job having to do with engines. Such an arrangement apparently fitted the needs of both man and company. There was little investment in each other. Despite his ostensible desire for new experiences, he was not ready to make any effort to obtain them. Instead, he was demanding from the organization more emotional support which was not forthcoming.

In this psychological contract there was the use of a pair of hands in return for the accrual of seniority. Neither party recognized that there was now more to the psychological contract. He was not satisfied with his relationships with other people nor did he find in his relationships with the company satisfying modes of coping with the changes in himself. Because the changed psychological contract was unfulfilled, the man had no enthusiasm. There was little to feel stimulated about. Reciprocation functioned minimally. He found few gratifications in his work.

By way of contrast, let us take a gas serviceman who was born and reared in the town where he worked. He came to the company looking for a job with a future.

I started with much less money than other jobs, with actually pretty low salary, but there is no chance for advancement in other jobs. [To him advancement meant "steady."] Well, I don't plan to stay here always, but I plan to advance with the company.

He said that he liked gas service because he met the public, and because he always tried to satisfy the public.

It is more or less a challenge to get ahead . . . it's a big kick to leave a home knowing they are pleased with you; I hate to think I would leave them with their not wanting to see me again. You sure have a challenge on your appliances. Each winter the companies come out with new things. Five years ago it was just furnaces. Now it's other things, like air conditioning units.

He became uncomfortable if he felt that he was overloaded with work, or if he was not doing his job as well as he could, as for example when getting a complaint on an appliance after he had fixed it. He noted that,

> I suppose years from now atomic energy will take over from gas and will be more automatic — you know, you push a button — but I don't think that will be in my lifetime.

In judging his income, he said he did not want to compare it with the incomes of those in another part of the company's operations. He preferred to compare it with those in another gas company. He said that he would move to another job if it paid more and if it were in the same area where he already had a home and friends and clubs to which he belonged.

This man saw opportunity and invested himself in the opportunity. He asked for and sought advancement, which for him was part of the contract. He took satisfaction in the advances in his industry, the experience of growth and change. He experienced neither loss nor imposed demand in change. He was able to project some of his values onto the company, for he required of the company that which he required of himself, namely that people be served well. He was able to satisfy some dependency needs by serving customers and being rewarded by them, needing therefore less reward from his supervisor. He saw more changes coming but he was not particularly threatened by them. When he compared himself with others, he chose, rationally, people who were in the same kind of business.

Already reciprocation was farther advanced than in the preceding example, for there was a spark of investment on his part and an anticipation that the company would invest in him. He saw what he did as challenge. He did not mention the interest of the authority figures from which we infer that the psychological distance between himself and his superiors was not as close as it might have been. This together with the fact that he had not experienced psychological stress on behalf of this organization would indicate that reciprocation, though operating reasonably well, was not at a particularly high level. As a result, it was not surprising this man should say that he would move to another job if it were to pay more. However, because other conditions for reciprocation were present, he and the company would likely have a mutually profitable and moderately rewarding relationship. He was finding many gratifications in his work, he was expanding his view of his capacities, and he was eager to make a productive contribution.

RECIPROCATION AND PRODUCTIVITY

Of those aspects of behavior indicative of mental health, reciprocation relates most closely to being active and productive. When reciprocation operates fully, it is essentially a productive process in three ways:

1. It makes the relationship of man and organization a productive one because it keeps the task as the central focus of the relationship and because they must work together to resolve personal and organizational conflicts related to the task.

2. It is productive for the individual. That is, as we have noted throughout, it contributes to the resolution of certain psychological conflicts, particularly those related to dependence, distance and change, and to the definition of an adult occupational identity. It increases the sources of gratification available to the individual, enabling him to draw more psychological sustenance from and to make more psychological investment in his environment.

3. It contributes to organizational productivity because, when it functions well, much of employees' energies are freed from having to deal with psychological conflicts related to the task and are then available to be invested in the task itself. This is not to say, however, that if people are freed from psychological conflicts they will invest all their energies in their work. Some work is so patently unsatisfying to most people that they simply can-

not invest themselves in it regardless of how much available energy they might have.

In addition to the many examples of increased sources of gratification we have cited, for many people, beyond the immediate goal of rearing a family, either there are no larger life purposes or what larger purposes there are seem impossible of fulfillment. In assuming the larger purposes and the goals of the company, one becomes a part of an entity which is larger than he is and through which he can contribute more to society than he might by himself. The company's aims and goals in part become the employee's aims and goals. But this is not altogether a one-way street, for as the employee remains in the organization over a period of time he has, ideally, greater freedom, independence, and maturity which enable him to be more creative.

Reciprocation broadens and makes more realistic his view of his own capacities, thereby enhancing his psychological growth. With a wider range of psychological supports and a greater amount of energy more readily available for his use, he has greater flexibility to deal with whatever stresses he may encounter. With less need to be preoccupied with himself and his own conflicts and to defend himself against possible threats, he is able to devote more of his attention to other people as individuals.

Reciprocation has another importance beyond its function as a productive process. As we indicated in chapter II, we "came upon" the concept of reciprocation. It arose as we tried to understand and organize our myriad experiences at Midland. Because reciprocation came to the fore in this way and made it possible to tie together what we had seen and heard, the importance of this concept to our study is self-evident.

But reciprocation is important beyond its heuristic value. We cannot understand behavior unless we come to some understanding of the processes which underlie it. Without a grasp of what gratifications people seek in their work and the process by which they try to attain them, we can act only in superficial trial and error fashion to provide sources of gratification which might enhance mental health.

So often, in fact, this is the way some have tried to foster mental health in industry. They have equated mental health with the "good life" and offered for both prescriptions and recipes. As a result, in the eyes of some people in management, efforts toward mental health have come to be equated with a sickly sweetness intended to make everyone happy. Such misconceptions also have led to programs to give employees various gifts "to make them happy" and in failure to confront and solve problems for fear of making people unhappy. These efforts fail, not only because they are misconceived, but also because they have little to do with mental health. They provide only a limited range of temporary gratifications. They resolve no conflicts.

The concept of reciprocation, however, provides us with an avenue to specify, examine, and ultimately to measure, forces related to mental health. Our understanding of reciprocation as a productive process becomes a point of departure for systematic efforts to promote mental health in the work place.

CHAPTER IX

THE RESOLUTION OF ORGANIZATIONAL CONFLICT

W_E have said that reciprocation is a productive process, in part because it is a process of conflict resolution for both the person and the company. We have discussed the importance of reciprocation for the resolution of conflicts about dependence, distance, and change. As we analyzed the components of reciprocation, we noted particularly the relationship of balanced distance to the variety of sources of gratification available to the person. We observed also the relationship of interdependence to psychological growth and of change to flexibility under stress. Seen another way, our discussion of interdependence highlighted joint expectations and joint productivity. Our analysis of distance emphasized individual expectations and personal productivity and the chapter on change weighted organizational expectations and organizational productivity more heavily.

In our discussion of reciprocation in chapter VIII we examined its conflict resolution function for the individual. Let us now examine in two examples its relationship to the resolution of organizational conflicts.

Conflict is a natural process which occurs in every formal organization simply because such an organization cannot be a homogeneous unit. Just as there are differences among individual people, so inevitably there are differences between parts of organizations. There are also problems between the organization and other organizations, regulatory bodies, communities, customers, and so on. In addition to the problems they pose for the organization, conflicts are "stressors," organizational conditions which create stress for the people involved. Reciprocation plays an important part in the resolution of both the "stressor" conflict and the resulting conflict for the individual.

Rivalry Between Units

Various units of a business organization tend to acquire their own specific points of view on both their work and the organization as a whole. Production, engineering, marketing, finance, et cetera — each has a tendency to see its function as most important and therefore to expect conformity to its needs and expectations from other units. There are many reasons for these views and expectations.

For one, people are recruited into respective units by the specialized nature of their work. There is a selective process, both on the part of the unit and the individual, which results in what might be described loosely as a "unit type." Sales executives often have a "salesman personality" in mind as they look for men. The terms "accounting personality" or "engineering personality" are frequently used in business circles to characterize personality types associated with typical occupational roles.

For another, there is customarily a degree of competition between units as each seeks to demonstrate its importance to the responsible authority figures, the company president and the board of directors.

Taken together, these factors contribute to distortions in perception, sometimes destructive competition, and, in extreme form, to a continuing flow of intraorganizational antagonism. When one unit seems to have attained an advantage, people in other units often feel that they must be less worthy and adequate. The values of a unit which gains ascendancy often threaten the values of another, for example, the "hard-boiled" production department may begrudge the time for "human relations" orientation which the personnel department advocates.

In a division of labor, required for organizational reasons, there are potential sources of conflict which can be extremely disruptive to the organization. They also can have a bearing on mental health as we have defined it.

At Midland, in addition to the usual functional divisions (accounting, engineering, merchandising) was the product division — gas and electric. In some parts of the organization there was conflict between these two divisions. This conflict was a "stressor" for some of the men in the gas division. These men were preoccupied with the differences between themselves and the electric men. Frequently they asked the researchers whether in other communities employees had brought up the feelings of rivalry between the two groups. Such a question almost never came from the electric men.

Electric work required more extensive training than gas. In communities where the company supplied both gas and electric services, promotion frequently was from work in the gas department to work in the electric department. All company trucks carried a decal which said, "Live Better Electrically." The members of the line crews saw themselves as the elite of the company. To observe them in their work, one had to look up. This symbolized the contrast between their work and that of the gas crews who worked mostly with pipe in the ground.

A young gas worker compared the relative prestige of gas and electric work as he felt it:

> Downtown, people see a man digging in the middle of the street during a blizzard and they say, "He must be a stupid sonofabitch." They see a man on a pole and they say, "He must know what he's doing." A lot of linemen feel they are better men because they are a lineman. You say you work for Midland Utilities and people say, "Line department?" and you say, "No," and they say, "Oh." It makes you feel kinda funny. Digging a ditch is the lowest form of work.

Given the differences in skill and experience, the men in nonsupervisory jobs in the gas operations were paid less on the average than those on the electric line crews. Where jobs in both services required the same skill and training, the wages were comparable, for example, meter readers, storekeepers. In recent years both groups had received the same percentage increases and the gas crews had received some special increases.

Gas operations tended to be concentrated in the less populous part of the state, in small communities with great distances between them, thus isolating the gas workers more from their own division headquarters, and from the general office in Shaw, than electrical workers. To complicate the problem, shortly before they were interviewed, the gas men lost their key management identification figure, Tim Watson.

A utility foreman, responsible for the work of several gas crews, told this story:

> . . . the Midland Utilities or the Telephone are the only ones to work for in this town for working standards and fair wages . . . I soon decided that electric business was not for me. You see [in military service], I saw some boys get hung up in hot wires. I believe that if a man is afraid of line work he should stay away from it . . . I know the gas business so I stick to that.
>
> I think that when someone is on the truck that you can trust to be decent to go into the house and render service with your wife, my wife, the kids there — he's worth a lineman's wage.

He went on to describe his interpretation of the attitudes of authority figures:

> . . . The Shaw people, they're primarily electric — and they don't get out to the properties — they relied on Mr. Watson to do that. They lost a wonderful man there when they lost him. Mr. ——— and Mr. ——— are both gas men, but, after all, Shaw runs this business, you know. ——— and ——— have been here only a few years. You can't pick up all this in a few years — I've been here fifteen and I'm still learning every day.
>
> As far as buying equipment and tools to do the job, they'll [the company] do anything for you on that. They couldn't be better. You only have to show why you need something and you will get it . . . Shaw probably has considerable to do with that — just like on the rolling stock.
>
> The union said we haven't been in the union long enough, we gas boys . . . The union representatives are all electric. They don't know

the gas industry and they don't make much attempt to find out about it. That's the way it looks to us. Mr. Watson fought for us and got us where we are today.

This, then, was a difficult problem, typical of business organizations. A major reason for the difficulty lay in the stretching of psychological distance to extremely uncomfortable proportions. Those gas men who were concerned saw themselves as less favored from the start. With more training, greater skill, and a self-described elite status, the electric men appeared to the gas men to be closer to other people both inside and outside of the company, a feeling reflected particularly in the remarks of the young gas worker ("Digging a ditch is the lowest form of work."). Being closer meant to the gas men that the electric men were held in greater affection and had more gratification from their work.

Society held the electric men in greater esteem and so did the company. Promotion was from gas to electric. The decals emphasized the contribution of electricity to better living, but not gas. The electric men generally were paid more. Furthermore, the gas men were usually geographically farther away from their supervisors which made for fewer contacts with superiors and less opportunity for approval and praise.

To those gas men who were concerned about the rivalry, it seemed that there was also less interdependence. If they believed they were not paid as adequately or esteemed as highly, they were saying in effect that the company did not need them as much as it needed the electric men. Then, change in the form of the loss of Watson represented a severe deprivation when in a sense they were under constant demand to maintain their self-esteem.

The loss of Watson interfered with reciprocation. They were, at least for the time being, without their major identification model. Whatever shaping of or acting upon the company they had done, they had done it through him. They no longer had this major support for their dependent needs, and for control and direction. Their "partner" was gone. Even though there was

a successor to Watson, they had not yet had enough time to identify themselves with him.

While the men were satisfied with many of the benefits the
company provided, they found it difficult to keep from contrasting their relative positions. The foreman continued:

. . . but they [the gas men] like the company . . . the eight hours
work, the regular pay check, and they have things like retirement an-
nuity, and sick benefits — there's a fringe benefit there that they
wouldn't get in a small outfit. They're getting that compensation but
not in dollars and cents. But then the linemen are getting the same
thing but the dollars and cents too.

A storekeeper who distributed supplies to both gas and electric
crews saw them from a relatively neutral position:

They more or less divide up into categories. The gas boys go with
the gas boys, and the electric goes with the electric . . . But me, I have
to associate with both the gas and electric. It's a difficult position sometimes — I hear all sides of it and I have to be neutral.

The resulting stress was shown in behavior as well as in comments of these gas personnel. The researchers noted that older,
less capable men on gas crews were more readily used as scapegoats and targets for the aggression of their fellow workers than
on electric crews.

In self defense the gas men resorted to mechanisms which made
it even more difficult to cope with the situation. Few gas men
admitted more training was required for electric work. They did
not recognize that frequently they gravitated to the kind of work
they had because they were ill prepared, either intellectually or
technically, to do much else. The men denied any personal responsibility for their unfavored position (for recognition of this
would be painful), and said their lot was poor solely because
they were gas men in an organization where gas was not domi-
nant.

Reciprocation was impaired, but not absent. They could talk
with each other about their common problem which helped them
balance their psychological distance from each other. Though

they did not think they were as highly esteemed as the electric men their jobs were often still the best in their communities. The good equipment which the company provided, showed that it could and did care about them. Some were able to recognize that their job was a responsible one, requiring care and caution; for them, such a feeling was a resource upon which to draw (interdependence).

The effects of diminished reciprocation on mental health were readily apparent. The single most vivid complaint of these gas men was that they had conspicuously fewer gratifications than the electric men. Their use of defense mechanisms which contributed nothing to the solution of their problem reflected their lack of flexibility in this stress situation. Their unrealistic view of themselves exaggerated their limitations and depreciated their assets. In stereotyping the electric men and management, and in making scapegoats of the older men on the crews, they were not treating these important others as individuals. Bound up as they were in their defensive maneuvers, they were not psychologically free to continue to develop themselves as they might have. By definition, they were not resolving their joint problem with the company nor was the company itself able to resolve it at this point.

The company faced several limitations in the solutions it could undertake. It had tried to treat the gas men as fairly as the electric men by giving them the same percentage increases. That there was a wage differential was an economic fact of life about which the company could do little: nationally the pay scales for gas men were lower than those for electric men. The company had anticipated the loss of Watson and had a replacement on the job when the loss occurred. Unfortunately it occurred before the men had come to know their new leader.

Conflict in the Community

In previous chapters we indicated there were close community ties for people at Midland. Not only did they have deep roots in their communities, but also management people particularly took an active part in community betterment projects. Thus conflict with the community which threatened loss of the company's franchise constituted a serious threat to the company and stress for the employees.

Up to a decade ago, such conflicts were not unusual in the utility business. As we noted in chapter VIII, in the early days of electricity many communities developed their own generating and transmission facilities. Some communities found them uneconomical and sold them to private utilities. Other communities were divided about the economic feasibility of building their own facilities versus permitting private utilities to do so. In still other communities, for political rather than economic considerations, the major question was whether utilities should be publically owned or investor owned. In any event, where there was a history of such differences, the issue tended to arise again whenever it was time to renew the franchise for the private utility.

Such a conflict occurred in two phases in the community of Maron, where a Midland division office was located. First there was an attempt to authorize a bond issue, the proceeds of which would be used to create municipally owned electric service. The bond issue was defeated in a municipal election. Several years later, when again there was some discussion in the community about a prospective bond election, a group within the community petitioned for an election to renew Midland's franchise. The company sent two management men to assist the local manager in his battle for survival. The election was won by those who favored the franchise. This issue, then, had twice placed Midland people in Maron in painful situations.

A division manager described the situation:

[A petition was started] where the citizens asked the mayor [actually the city council] to grant the power company a franchise. If that is signed by 20 percent of the electors, the mayor and councilmen go ahead and arrange the franchise or give the people a chance to vote on it. The way it worked here, the mayor and council never signed the franchise at all. They put it to a vote and we won so that the agreement with the power company was made over the heads of the mayor and council. It's disappointing to have a mayor and a couple of commissioners against the power company that way.

It was as if the mayor and commissioners were against him personally. He then attributed the blame for the conflict to consulting engineers who, he alleged, "stirred up these fights."

. . . they tell them, "First thing you need is a survey, and then if you decide eventually that you need some electrical construction and want to run your own system, I will get three percent as your consultant." Then he goes into some kind of a trance and of course he comes up saying: "Yes, the city should build its own light plant." Of course if they don't build a light plant, he isn't going to get any money. You'd be surprised how few people see through that. He had 'em all convinced here that they were going to make a big profit.

A woman clerk in the division office described conflict as she experienced it:

That franchise was a dirty battle here. It was based on a lot of dirty lies. People were making accusations about the company, but if you asked them for proof they couldn't possibly back it up. They would get up at meetings and say that the company's going to lay off a bunch of men as soon as they got the franchise. [The manager] was wonderful. He said that he would keep the payroll here and he did. A lot of people ignored him up and down the street — [the manager] and us in here — they weren't very friendly. But the farmers were fighting for Midland. We serviced the rurals. They wanted us here because if we had been thrown out of Maron they would have had to send [men] from Soton [a town twenty miles away] if there were any trouble. We try to take care of the customer.

My husband was in business here at the time. He was more or less between the devil and the deep blue sea. People wanted to know how he stood. He was making a living off the customers in town. He wouldn't voice his opinion — he had a lot of pro and con. He did say that he had a lot of trouble with power failures but anytime he called the company they were always right down there to correct the trouble. A few business men were cold to him but it didn't hurt the business any as far as we could tell. I always figure that if you fight fair and square you will win out. Lying or cheating won't get you anywhere.

Another woman clerk, then working for the company in a neighboring community, mentioned the franchise fight spontaneously in the interview. By doing so several years after the last event, she indicated the degree of stress it had held for her:

... there was a lot of mud slinging at the time. There was practically fist fights in some of those meetings. People criticized the girls who worked there. They were saying they were always out for coffee and things like that ... There were people in town who had rental property who wouldn't rent to Midland employees. One merchant told me that a local contractor's wife was trying to get him not to vote for Midland. She was a very good customer of his. She had never been back in the store since Midland got the franchise — he told her that he thought it was the best thing for the town to keep the company.

Another perspective was offered by an engineer who said:

I went through the elections there at Maron. The town was flooded with propaganda. About 30 percent were wrought up. The others went along with their friends. When the election was held, we had a majority (two percent) of the votes cast. It was a matter of friendship. Some people and their friends voted for municipal service and others were for the utility. There was a matter of public versus private enterprise ... Everyone in the company, of course, felt involved. It was bread and butter. However, if the company lost the election, I knew that I would be moved in my job. The linemen had more reason to be worried. They thought they would have to work for the city. So they regarded a vote for municipal as a personal insult ... We had a big meeting of all the company employees and ... each of us volunteered to take names of people we knew. Our job was to be impersonal and just to approach people, not with the attitude of finding out how they were going to vote but just to get an opportunity to tell our side of the story. As I recall it, I took 12 or 14 people.

The company had to resolve this conflict in order to survive in the community. That it did so was due in no small measure to reciprocation. As was evident in these quotations, its people identified their interests with those of the company and took an active part in defending the company's position. What had gone on before, together with the steps the company took to defend itself, enhanced reciprocation. Although the employees had already rallied around the manager, whom they described as "wonderful," when the company sent in two other executives to help, these men served as additional identification figures to support their dependency needs. The coming of these two men said in effect to the employees that the company had affection for them because it cared enough about what was happening to them to give them this added strength. Thus at a time when they were becoming increasingly distant from some people in the community they could come closer to each other and stand united with the company in coping with this drastic change.

An important instrument toward this cohesion was the common value system prevalent in the company. The reaffirmation of such values as "honesty" and "fairness" and "free enterprise," previously stressed by the company, re-emphasized their common bond.

Both interdependence and balanced distance were maintained, and there was mutual coping with change. While they had already suffered some psychological loss ("there were people in town . . . who wouldn't rent to Midland employees") and they were faced with increased demands in the form of the need to defend themselves, because reciprocation continued to function, they were able to meet the threat head on.

Conditions for reciprocation were largely maintained despite the threat. Employees did have an area of freedom in which to function; they could talk to people individually and present their side of the story. In a similar situation another company might well have forbidden its employees to enter into discussions or arguments and insisted that only officials speak on behalf of the company. The employees, as we have already noted, had strong identification figures who accepted and supported their dependency needs. They were confronting the stress together with their leaders and the larger company. They had a feeling of fair share partnership with the company.

While we have so far indicated that reciprocation served to cushion the stress for the employees, the stress did begin to interfere with reciprocation as some of the quotations indicated. The employees were deprived of some of their gratifications as people in the community turned on them (". . . there was a lot of mud slinging" . . . "People criticized the girls" . . . "There were people who . . . wouldn't rent to Midland employees"). Friendships were destroyed; anger and fear were stimulated. Midland people felt themselves being manipulated or unfairly attacked.

These attacks in turn tended to make employees depreciate themselves in their own eyes. It was not easy for them to maintain self-images as good people who rendered valuable public service, when at least a segment of the community was telling them in many ways that they were no good. To a certain extent the attacks also made it difficult to treat others as individuals. Being under stress their natural reaction was to classify people into those who were for the company and those who were against the company. Their opponents were viewed as telling "a lot of dirty lies," being cold and unfriendly, indulging in "mud slinging" — in short, as being "the enemy." While much of this perspective may have been accurate, stereotyping people in this way would tend to make it difficult to understand why they behaved as they did and to deal with their behavior with psychological rationality.

Obviously such a situation began to interfere with ordinary productivity. The extra tension which people carried from day to day would inevitably have some effect on their efficiency at work and would drain some energy from ordinary activity to deal with the emergency.

But more important, in a situation in which the company could reasonably have slighted its employees to concentrate all its efforts on the community, it did not do so. Its attention to the employees not only served to relieve some of their stress, but strengthened the company's hand as well. Thus, reciprocation contributed significantly to the resolution of a critical organizational conflict.

The resolution of personal conflicts, however, was not complete. Long after the battle had been won, there was still an undercurrent of tension among some of the employees.

The engineer reported that "public relations" contacts had tended to be one-sided, with the company *bending over backward* (italics ours). The division manager developed an attitude of "keeping the customer happy at any cost," which created conflicts for employees in the company. Even the phrase, "bending over backward" described an imbalance, an uncomfortable position.

On occasion employees in both Maron and Soton complained about being under-cut by their superiors to please the customer. People were granted special favors or, by special public relations arrangements with the manager, were allowed to be delinquent in their bills beyond the usual deadline set by the company. This seeming favoritism increased the psychological distance between employees and manager, and decreased interdependence. When they felt the manager was undercutting them, he was no longer providing them support for their dependency needs or maintaining the sense of partnership or providing consistent controls. His behavior therefore fostered feelings of hostility which now had no constructive outlets. Hence there were some continuing unresolved conflicts for the employees. Reciprocation was being undone.

Some conflict and tension are inevitable in organizational life. However, it appears that chronic and destructive conflict can be minimized. In fact, reciprocation appears to grow as man and company work together toward resolving conflict.

CHAPTER X

TOWARD ACTION

THE purpose of this study was to come to a better understanding of the relationship between work and mental health. To do so, we tried to understand some of the forces which operate within people's personalities which in turn lead to fundamental psychological needs. In the last analysis, it is fundamental needs with which we must deal if we are to grasp the depths of people's feelings.

Our study took us into two areas. People told us of some of their needs in the form of expressing their common concerns about their work. By doing so they also repeated for us a major psychological truth: that to maintain psychological equilibrium, to gratify one's needs, one must constantly resolve the conflicts which arise between the internal demand for need gratification and the external controls society imposes upon the ways in which needs may be gratified. That is, the process of need gratification is always a process of conflict resolution. Maturity and wisdom are built up out of successive, effective resolutions of conflict.

We have seen that people come to work in a business organization with the unexpressed (usually unconscious) intention of resolving conflicts here as they must in every other sphere of life. The concepts we have advanced to describe these conflicts would seem to encompass a range of experiences which are highly important to mental health in industry. No consideration of the relationship of work to mental health can safely omit the significance of the phenomena we have conceptualized as the psychological contract. Nor can the concerns with interdependence, balanced distance and change be disregarded. According to our discussion, these concepts would seem to fit together in this fashion:

Because this is an exploratory study, we must still regard much of our discussion of these concepts as hypothesis. In time, we may come to give greater or lesser emphasis to one or another of them. Perhaps we will evolve more or different concepts and therefore reorganize our thinking along somewhat different lines. Meantime, we will have to develop ways of measuring dependence, distance, the stress of change, and reciprocation. We will have to devise methods of ascertaining the expectations of both people and companies, particularly those which are less conscious and more obscure, for these, ultimately, will become important factors in the process of selecting employees and making clear the psychological contract. Common agreement on the psychological contract at the beginning of a relationship will come to be even more important in many ways than agreement on the legal contract. When the psychological contract is not fulfilled, the effects are not as readily counteracted by such measures as collective bargaining as are differences about the legal contract.

These tasks for research will concern the professional investigator. The management reader, who is essentially an empiricist, will prefer two other directions. He, too, can pursue a kind of "research." That is, dealing with people and their problems at work, as he does, he will be in a position to compare our observations and conclusions with his own. Second, he will want to know what he can do to enhance reciprocation and thereby to foster mental health.

WHAT THE EXECUTIVE CAN DO

The Executive as a Preventive Agent

Just as the business executive must keep a constant eye on his profit margin, his inventory, and other material aspects of his business, if he is to anticipate and avoid difficulties, so he must constantly study psychological factors in that part of the business for

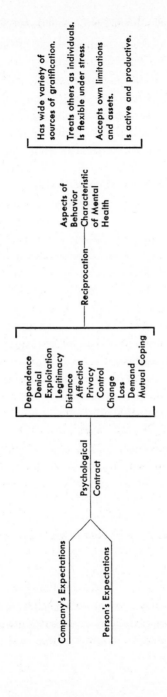

Company's Expectations

Person's Expectations

Psychological
Contract

Dependence
Denial
Exploitation
Legitimacy
Distance
Affection
Privacy
Control
Change
Loss
Demand
Mutual Coping

Reciprocation

Aspects of
Behavior
Characteristic
of Mental
Health

Has wide variety of
sources of gratification.

Treats others as individuals.
Is flexible under stress.

Accepts own limitations
and assets.

Is active and productive.

which he is responsible. In particular, he will need to create and maintain the conditions for reciprocation in his unit. He will want to be certain that people can plan some of their own work and contribute their ideas to the larger goals of the organization. He will want supervisors at every level to understand their role as identification figures and the necessity for accepting dependency needs. Both he and his subordinates will need to recognize that fair share partnership between superiors and subordinates does not mean a relationship without controls, nor does it mean that an exchange of money for services is an adequate base for a partnership.

The second step in anticipating and avoiding problems is to try to assess at the time of employment some of the psychological needs the prospective employee will seek to meet in his work. Is the young man asking the company to help him find himself? If so, where in the organization is there a wise, mature supervisor to whom he can be assigned? Does this woman seek a job because she really needs the money or is she looking to work as a way of enriching her relationships with other people? If she comes to the company for the latter, is there a work group in which she can be placed where there is an informal exchange during the day as contrasted with an isolated position on an assembly line? What are the company's unstated expectations? How will a man's performance be judged? How much is the company expecting him to change? How do the two sets of expectations fit together?

Few personnel interviewers will immediately be capable of making such judgments accurately and there are not as yet psychological inventories adequate to help them do so. If, however, they are thinking in this direction, that is one step toward making better judgments. Hopefully, judgments will improve with time and experience.

It should be recognized, however, that even when serious and consistent effort is given to providing opportunities for the gratification of psychological needs, these opportunities will not always necessarily lead to mentally healthy behavior. A person himself, for his own reasons, may not be able to take advantage of the opportunities for gratification. Various other actions on the part of the company may serve to deny gratifications from these potential sources. When, for example, there are unresolved organizational conflicts which induce stress for the individual, the person is left helpless to confront the issues. The problems seem insurmountable and incapable of being resolved by what seem to him his own inadequate resources. Not only are possible gratifications lost, but the person must also carry an added psychological burden.

Ideally, though, when a person becomes part of a business organization, he can accept as part of himself the strength and power of the company. In many stressful situations therefore he can bear more stress than he might be able to handle alone. So it is that work associations under optimum conditions can result in greater psychological strength.

The Executive as a Diagnostic Agent

It is an axiom in business circles that there is no such thing as perfect preventive maintenance. This axiom is as true about people as it is about machines. Despite the best of preventive efforts, difficulties and problems will arise. Sometimes these will not be clearly evident. At other times, if the problem is an organizational conflict, the executive may feel that not all "stressor" or organization conflict is sufficiently threatening to the organization to require managerial efforts toward its resolution. Some conflicts which may seem too insignificant for organizational action may nonetheless have destructive effects on mental health. If the executive is to be concerned about mental health, he will need to sharpen his sensitivity to subtle, early indicators of stress and, at the same time, he will need to counteract the tendency to dismiss as unimportant conflicts which do not have a "four-alarm" quality.

In our discussion we have pointed out various kinds of behavior which were manifestations of underlying stress. In a word, stress which interferes with reciprocation and the smooth psychological functioning of a person reflects itself in behavior which is more primitive and less productive than is otherwise possible for the people involved. Such behavior can be classified under four headings. These, in turn, can serve as a diagnostic guide.

Hostile Feelings. Expressions of hostility are the most widely recognized signs of conflict. In our examples we have seen a number of such expressions. In chapter IV, when the manager could not accept dependency needs, there was widespread, open criticism of the employees among the middle management. The employees flouted authority and were passively resistant, in addition to quarreling among each other. The second group of women in chapter V vehemently expressed their anger toward their supervisor. Of course, hostility was most blatant in chapter IX, when employees who ordinarily had positive feelings about their friends, neighbors, and customers became angry with some of these same people. We would suggest then, that when expressions of hostility appear in the form of sharp outbursts or chronic repetitive behavior, these indicate strong underlying conflict.

Loss of Control. The conflict is more severe when expressions of hostility become increasingly open and uncontrolled. In the Maron example in chapter IX, there were open name-calling, criticism, and nasty remarks, but more important, people were refused homes and others refused to patronize merchants whose opinions differed from their own. The second group of women in chapter V spoke of the office as being in a "constant uproar." In the first example in chapter IV there was open quarreling between those who wanted to establish a structure and others who felt the former were taking over.

Overuse of Defenses. The use of defenses is a subtle matter and somewhat harder to observe than hostile reactions. Among some of the gas men in chapter IX, denial was an important defense. Some of them could not let themselves perceive accurately some of the realities of their situation. Those who denied some of the reasons for the conflict could not begin to deal with conflict;

instead they dissipated much of their energy flaying straw men as did those gas men who saw electric men as their opponents.

Another mechanism is withdrawal. We saw this with the Elders in chapter VI, and in a different form with the second group of women in chapter V. In one case the men withdrew from the new job and in the other case the women withdrew from each other.

In chapter IV some of the middle management attributed the problems to the union. This is a form of projection, shifting the blame to the union, which provided them with some "rational" explanation for behavior they could not understand.

Helplessness. The most conspicuous expression of helplessness came from the middle management man in chapter VIII who equated himself with three old trucks. Among some of the gas men in chapter IX there was a feeling of helplessness, as there was among the supervisors in chapter IV, who looked to the researchers for ways of coping with their problems.

The executive who will attune himself to these indications of conflict will then be able to take the initiative in dealing with the conflict before it assumes imperative proportions.

The Executive as a Remedial Agent

Our discussion provides us with examples of specific steps which relieved or prevented stress. In some situations stress might have been anticipated or diminished. Using the latter examples, and having the advantage of hindsight, we will suggest some possible steps that might have been taken. We will make best use of our examples by abstracting principles from them. These principles, according to our discussion, would seem to be useful guides for the executive who must resolve organizational conflicts and alleviate stress.

Principle 1. Basic to the successful tolerance of and coping with stress in an organization is a firm relationship with the organization — the effective functioning of reciprocation.

Whenever there is a conflict which makes for stress, the tendency of most people is to rush in to seek immediate and direct relief of the symptom without thinking about the fact that there is an underlying problem to be solved. The executive must therefore, as a first step, strengthen the people who are under stress. This makes it easier for them to cope with the conflict while he comes to understand the basic reason for the conflict and evolves long-range solutions. In Maron (chapter IX), the company devoted considerable attention to its people, despite the external pressures. This made it possible to mount a stronger, more united defense and to cushion some of the stress for the employees.

In the situation of the Elders (chapter VI), where the men had suffered a psychological loss while at the same time new demands were being made of them, several steps could have been taken which would have avoided much of the experience of loss and created an experience of mutual coping with change. For example, the plant superintendent might have met with the Elders (or with all of the men for that matter), and have made it possible for them to express their fear, anxiety, and anger. He might then have set up different training programs, one for the Elders and another for the Heirs. One program would have been slower, more personal, and, hopefully, taught by an older man (best by the superintendent himself). By patient demonstration and repetition, plus the opportunity for identification, the Elders probably could have learned more easily, with less of a feeling of loss. Their historic relationship to the company could have been maintained and they would probably have felt less stress.

The leader in chapter IV who told his subordinate, "You've got to go to a certain place on a certain day . . . the boys know you are coming," knew intuitively that the leader must constantly be building the relationship of the men to the organization by accepting dependency needs. To do this the leader had to be with the men, even if there were no specific problems for him to deal with.

Principle 2. In each conflict situation, fundamental to the alleviation of stress and the resolution of a problem is the opportunity to identify oneself with one or more key authority figures.

We have already indicated the importance of identification, particularly during a stressful period, to the Elders. In chapter IV, the employees had no strong identification figures. Given the fact that this particular manager (for reasons we have not discussed to protect anonymity) could not have become such a figure, that stress could not be resolved until a new leader had been designated.

The gas men in chapter IX had recently lost a supportive authority who could both relieve them of much of their concern with their problem and do something toward its solution. Before this conflict could be resolved a new identification figure would have to establish himself with the men. They could talk with such a person about the problem. Though concerned about their welfare and progress, he would have to point out certain aspects of reality, for example, gas men *were* in less demand, they *were* less skilled. He would then press the more realistic aspects of their case with higher management. Underlying all of his acts would have to be the subtle communication to the men that he was in fact *their* strong leader and that he had affection for them.

In Maron, the company strengthened an already effective leader by sending in others who also were recognized as leaders to help him and his unit. The employees derived considerable psychological support from this move. They had more power to cope with the situation because by identifying themselves with the new leaders they in effect assumed some of the strength of the leaders. A similar move to support the new leader in the "Loss of a Leader" example in chapter IV would have been advantageous.

Principle 3. Management action toward the solution of a problem unites employees to combat the problem at hand, rather than letting them spend their energies in excessive defense activities.

We noted particularly that the second group of women in chapter V, and the people in the first example of chapter IV, dissipated much of their energies in protecting themselves. The same was true, but less conspicuously so, in several other examples. One of the men in the chapter IV example said, "I'd rather have them come down and give me a good chewing than not to come down at all." Another said, "They don't come around and try to understand our plight . . ."

When management openly recognizes a problem, when it tries to understand a problem as the employees experience it, and particularly when it mobilizes the employees to help in the solution of the problem, each of these steps decreases stress. People then more easily "let their guard down." They begin to make more constructive use of their energies and no longer feel the conflict to be threatening to them. Maron is again a case in point.

Principle 4. Resolution of a conflict is incomplete if subsequent efforts to avoid further conflicts become overcompensations.

Overcompensation creates new stress by undermining interdependence, and disrupting the balance of psychological distance between employees and superiors. The employees may then see their bosses as having more affection for others than for themselves and as undercutting them to please others.

The conflict in Maron began to subside when the bond election issues were decided. With time, the proximity of people, and the necessity for their working together in the interest of their community, it might have been expected that residuals of conflict would gradually disappear. When, however, in an effort to hurry the healing process, the manager began to grant special favors, he created resentment among his employees. The employees could only wonder why they should bend over backward when they had only defended their legitimate interests.

If overcompensation appears in the form of "buying off" the employees because of some guilt feelings on the part of management, this, too, disrupts the partnership because it substitutes guilt-motivated behavior for actions designed to resolve conflicts or to enhance reciprocation.

If, in the situation in chapter IV in which a man lost his arm, the company had gone to great lengths beyond honest adjudication to "pacify" the men, the men would have felt either that they had been done a greater injustice than they had thought at first or the company was an easy mark. The latter feeling would have been destructive to reciprocation because it would have indicated that the company was not a strong partner.

The Executive as an Iatrogenic Agent

In medicine the word iatrogenic refers to symptoms or illnesses caused by the physician himself in the course of his treatment of the patient. Many problems in industry which the executive is called upon to solve are of his own making though he may be unaware of their origin, as was the manager in chapter IV. In carrying out these multiple roles of prevention, diagnosis, and correction, the executive will therefore need to maintain two foci:

a. He must constantly be aware of his own influence on the behavior of his subordinates. His will be the single most important influence on those whom he supervises in the course of their work. This is not to imply that each individual person is not shaped by parental and cultural influences in the course of his development. Nor is it to say that there are not many other influences on adults outside of the work place. It is to say that when people are together for a work task the influence of the leader is paramount.

b. He must look upon the relationship of each man to his company as a process. That is, events and behavior flow from one another into one another. There is no such thing as a single cause and a single consequence. The relationship of a man to his company is constantly being affected one way or another, not alone at contract time or by the specific effect, now and then, of a change in work conditions or fringe benefits. Perhaps a good analogy to what the executive must do is the weatherman's constant study of the many forces upon which he bases his predictions. Only in this way can the executive really begin to understand what is going on and only in this way can he avoid the use of futile gimmicks.

THE FUTURE

Management's Concern

For some years, many managements have been concerned about mental health, but their concern (and that of professionals) has been a narrow one. In the 1954 survey of mental health in industry referred to in the Preface, we found that what limited discussion there was in the literature about mental health in industry placed heavy emphasis on the individual. Such phrases as, "The pathological emotional attitude of employees . . ." and "industrial psychopathy" indicated that the writers saw many of the mental health problems in industry as the "fault" of the individual. The statistics available had to do with absenteeism, accidents, and alcoholism, with the frequent implication that such symptoms arose independently of the job itself. It was said, for example, and unfortunately we repeated it, that only five per cent of sickness absenteeism was due to on-the-job causes.

With such a heavy emphasis on the pathological condition of the individual, something needed to be done about him and his problems. No matter where the "fault" lay, the price to industry was still high and therefore industry had to do something about it. Some managements tried to do something in the form of psychiatric, psychological, and counseling programs for people whose personal problems interfered with their work. These emotional first-aid efforts served, and still serve, an important purpose, but they are limited both in their conception of how emotional problems arise and what can be done about them. They offer little direction for the possibility of preventing at least some of these problems.

Furthermore, the steps which might be taken toward fostering mental health in industry are not solely the function of medical departments, personnel departments, or researchers. This does not mean that the effects of work on mental health (and mental health on work, for that matter) are not the legitimate concern of these departments and of academic research on industrial human relations. But the matter of work and mental health is too important for *organizational reasons* to be regarded as of less than central importance by management. Managerial decisions and managerial actions are crucial to reciprocation.

Though we do not know to what degree mental health correlates with economic efficiency, or even whether it should, it is obvious from some of the examples we have offered that behaviors which are the antitheses of mental health are also often neither personally nor economically productive. Furthermore, reciprocation can hardly be denied, despite anyone's attempts to do so, without an economic price.

It follows, then, that the business organization, in addition to its economic function, has a contribution to make to the mental health of its people — without becoming a clinic or an occupational therapy shop. Mental health is not a matter of managerial concern because it is humanitarian to have such an interest or because it is believed to be "good for" employee or public relations. Such an essentially "employee benefit" view of mental health is based on a rarely examined assumption: that "good human relations" is one thing and "getting the job done" is another. The manager often sees these as contradictory objectives, and regrets his inability to pursue both objectives simultaneously.

This study has been a beginning step toward a comprehensive program of mental health in industry, and, hopefully, toward the prevention of mental illness. It is part of a new but growing tradition. It offers some ideas and concepts, many of which will need to be examined and tested in research and practice. If its explicit purpose was to explore and examine, to understand better, then its implicit purpose was to lay a groundwork for further study.

The industrial milieu is both a critical and a fertile field for such a study. It offers extremely rich possibilities of collaboration between management, labor, and researchers in the interests of the psychological well-being of people. There are lessons to be learned in every office and every shop. We hope that other far-sighted executives will offer their organizations for study as did the chief executive of Midland. Given such cooperation, we can expect a flurry of studies and wider interest in mental health in industry as psychiatry and psychology move from treatment to prevention and as management develops broader understanding of mental health.

But study is not enough. What is learned in research must be applied. This will require professional people who are trained to help bring about useful change in business organizations (as differentiated from making recommendations). Few people have had experience in bringing about such changes. Even fewer are being formally trained to do so. In its own self-interest, as well as that of its people, management will have to demand people with such skills and support teaching programs which will prepare them. In too many instances staff studies and consultants' reports gather dust on shelves because there is no one to help manage-ment put their recommendations into practice. The same fate will befall research on industrial mental health unless provisions are made to translate research results into action.

One step in the application of knowledge about mental health is the education of management and labor leadership. Seminars which communicate such knowledge and which help develop familiarity with mental health concepts are already becoming popular. There are clinically trained people in many communities — psychiatrists, clinical psychologists, psychiatric social workers — as well as those in university and psychiatric settings, who can conduct such seminars. They will need to be encouraged and invited to do so. One model has been developed in The Menninger Foundation seminars for executives and occupational physicians. The National Association for Mental Health has published a guide, derived from this model, for conducting seminars in local communities. Dr. Harry Wagenheim in the Department of Psy-chiatry of Temple University and Dr. P. J. Sparer in the Department of Psychiatry of the University of Tennessee have developed other models. Although not intended to be related to mental health, group dynamics experiences sponsored by the National Training Laboratories are another useful model.

Some companies are using psychiatric and psychological consultants for teaching mental health concepts. A few have clinically trained people on their own staffs, an important part of whose function is education, particularly of management. The work of Dr. Alan McLean at IBM, Dr. Ralph Collins at Eastman Kodak, and Dr. James Conant at General Electric (Hanford) are examples. There will be many more such programs when management interest becomes sufficiently serious to train people for them.

Uncommon Sense

No doubt there will be many who think that talk about mental health in industry is so much blather. Some will question any expression of management interest in mental health. They will view such interest as management's seeking another device to manipulate people.

Some among management will scorn their colleagues who express an interest in mental health. There are the men who will say that human relations efforts in industry have failed, that a concern for the health of people is a form of "softness" not appropriate in industry. If, however, we look closely into situations where human relations practices are alleged to have failed, we see invariably that what passed for human relations was manipulation. The allegation really means that those who sought to manipulate others failed in the effort, and when the psychological confidence game failed, they gave up altogether. Psychological *understanding* cannot fail. Although there is yet much to be learned and understood, there is already a significant body of psychological and social science knowledge. Management fails when it tries to substitute make-believe for the understanding which can come from this knowledge.

To think psychologically, to be concerned about the mental

health of people, requires, in Dr. Karl Menninger's words, "uncommon sense." It requires a look beneath the surface of the obvious to the feelings of one's fellow man. Many have said that human beings should serve social institutions. The person who thinks psychologically will add that social institutions should serve human beings.

RESEARCH TEAM OPERATIONS

THE purpose of this appendix is to provide for clinical and social science colleagues, as well as other interested readers, a more detailed account of the concepts and methods of the Midland study.

Background of the Study

The pilot investigation which we have reported in this book was of course preceded by numerous developments in theory, research, and application, carried on by many people from various professional disciplines. Some of these efforts are loosely grouped under the rubric of "Social Psychiatry." Social psychiatric theory includes the perspectives of the cultural anthropologist and those of the investigator in psychosomatic medicine. Social psychiatric research has ranged from studying the effects of various rehabilitation techniques on alcoholics to compiling statistics on instances of combat breakdown in war. Action programs in social psychiatry include the therapeutic use of group dynamics in organizations as well as marriage counseling and mental hospital reform.

It would seem that any and every concern with the relationship between people and their environment — regarding as relevant all levels of personality functioning and all dimensions of social and cultural process — has been considered at one time or another by those who said they were committed to a social-psychiatric approach.

In a review of the field, Leighton, Clausen, and Wilson (19) suggest four issues which seem to have been involved in most of the investigations and action programs which have been called socio-psychiatric. They are: a concern with concepts of normality and abnormality; a concern with relationship between the social environment and personality development, defining "chances for health" as one aspect of human maturation; the implications of cultural and cross-cultural diversity for effective understanding and prevention of mental illness;

the effects of mental illness on the social environment, that is, the modes of the societal reaction to illness.

Some conclusions from this large variety of previous work formed a background for our own research efforts. Our review of the literature indicated that:

a. Who is defined as sick and who is defined as well varies from group to group, class to class, and culture to culture in human society. Many studies have noted that the same behavioral phenomena may be viewed as evidence of illness in one setting but not in another.

b. The term "mental health" itself masks many complexities in human functioning which should be recognized rather than denied or oversimplified. Inevitably mental health is affected by the total personality of an individual and the total environmental context within which that individual functions. Scientists feel at a loss to cope with this complexity because they are accustomed to making distinctions between mind and body, between individual and society, between intrapersonal and interpersonal phenomena.

c. Scientific understanding of relationships between social process and individual functioning is difficult to achieve because we do not know which variables are most relevant to a definition of the problem. No general theory of human behavior — linking social process and psychological process in an integrated system — has yet evolved (13).

d. Work has been less intensively studied from a mental health point of view than has the family setting, or relationships between the person's position in the total social system to his propensity for mental illness.

e. Management, while increasingly committed to the maintenance of physical health within the organizations of business and industry, has been somewhat reluctant to become involved in a concern with psychological health, feeling in many cases that such a concern would exceed management's responsibility. Meanwhile, the clinical professions have found it difficult to develop a "public health" point of view which could be applied specifically in work situations, and social science researchers on human behavior at work have rarely approached their task from a background of interest in the prevention of psychological illness or the maintenance of mental health. The concern on the part of both industrial managements and researchers in industry usually has been with "human relations," morale, and the various aspects of work life which have an effect on organizational and work performance.

Yet the efforts of a number of investigators and practicing clinicians since World War I laid the groundwork for the more intensive concern with problems of psychological health and illness at work which is now becoming evident. The principal names and dates in this historical development have been summarized by McLean and Taylor (24). In this historical background the work of Dr. William C. Menninger (during World War II) as Director, Neuropsychiatry Consultants Division, Office of The Surgeon General, U.S. Army, was most relevant to our concern at The Menninger Foundation. After the war, Dr. Menninger had maintained that preventive techniques should be developed in industrial situations which would draw upon the experience that had been gained in attempting to prevent psychological breakdown among the military personnel during World War II (26).

Clinicians and clinical researchers in industry, quite naturally, focused upon pathology. Some things have been learned in the last two decades about the prevalence of psychopathology among working populations. These studies demonstrate that psychological difficulties are not randomly distributed throughout the working population and, as would be expected, the relationships between circumstances at work and at home could serve either to enhance a person's possibilities of maintaining good mental health or combine to increase the probability that symptoms of illness would occur.

However, clinicians found it difficult to translate their knowledge gained in a treatment center to broader aspects of life such as the world of work. On the other hand, people with responsibility for management, supervision, and counseling in work settings, as well as social scientists interested in industrial life, had not included in their training an appreciation of what had been learned by clinicians about human motivation and behavior.

An exception to these generalizations is the work of investigators at the Tavistock Institute in Great Britain. Elliott Jaques, for example, (17), recognizes that both individual and organization are involved in an interplay and that efforts in the direction of prevention and improved human relations cannot be focused exclusively on either one of these elements in a situation. The same point of view had been implied in general terms some years before in another essay by a British clinician, Halliday (15), whose perspective included both the industrial organization and the community.

Another important series of industrial studies which served as background for our own efforts were the extensive researches, conducted in the United States, on relationships between productivity, supervision, and morale and other variables of concern to industrial management and personnel specialists. Much of this work has been carried on at the University of Michigan, where the Survey Research Center has conducted large-scale studies in more than a score of industries. These researchers have shown the important influence of supervisors' attitudes on worker performance, and have also emphasized the effects of technological change on interpersonal relations and morale in industry (22).

But these findings only accelerated the quest for specific efforts that could be undertaken to develop preventive programs in work settings. It was widely recognized that the approach of single disciplines would be less likely to produce these ideas for prevention than would an interdisciplinary approach. Each of the relevant fields had information that the others needed.

Confronted with these varying approaches in studies of mental health and human relations, we felt that our first step should be one of bridge-building. As we have explained in chapter II, the value of each of the approaches which had been developed by other researchers had somehow to be capitalized upon, while at the same time we needed to recognize that in our exploratory studies such terms as "personality" and "work environment" had to be defined as broadly as possible. We decided that our first step should be as "open-ended" a study as we could make in one specific industrial organization. We would seek to understand its culture, its reputation, its habitual work practices and policies, the kinds of people who enter such an organization and how they might contrast with others entering other kinds of employment, the day-to-day work activity and the meaning of this activity to the people involved, how people dealt with work-related stress and the consequences of these reactions to stress for the subsequent work experiences of individual organizational members. We would be interested in the interplay of organizational structure, group experience, and individual motives and defenses in determining the behavior of people at work and the meaning of work experience to them. We hoped that such an investigation, and others to follow, would enable us to specify, with greater clarity than had been possible in the past, features of work life which need to be taken into account from a mental health point of view, and *how* these various features should be related to each other. The Midland study, then, was our first step along this road.

Field Work

We started at Midland by first attempting to "get around" the entire organization in a series of visits to the communities and plants where company people worked, some forty different work locations. We began this first tour by explaining to management from top executives to first level supervisors what we proposed to do. We explained that we were in the company to learn, and not to diagnose. We were there to collaborate with them in learning about the relationship of work to a man's well being, not to offer free advice to the company or to find out who was sick. We touched briefly upon some of the previous findings in the area of work and mental health described above. We said we would be with people on the job as well as interviewing them privately. This same message was repeated to employees at the various company locations. (See appendix II for the text of this orientation talk.)

These brief visits gave us a quick appreciation of the many different kinds of work situations existing in this one organization. At the same time, they served the important purpose of introducing the researchers to company people, providing the opportunity for questions to be asked, and establishing closer contacts than would have been possible by formal speeches or announcements in company publications alone. At this early stage in the study, we hoped to resolve problems of sampling and research design, particularly by deciding which people or situations should be studied more intensively and which would safely be given less attention, while still maintaining a representative picture of work life in the organization.

But there were no guides available from theory for what sampling criteria we should use. We did not yet have grounds for hypothesizing which differences — age, sex, work location, size of work group, community context — would have the greatest significance for mental health. To devise a sample in terms of any combination of these criteria or others might mask other variables which would turn out to be crucial. We resolved the sampling problem by adopting a continuation of the clinical strategy with which we had begun.

The clinical method is essentially an inductive method. The investigator or therapist observes (usually on more than one occasion) his human subject (usually an individual person). As similar content or sequences of action appear again and again during these observations, the data begin to be interpreted by the observer as manifestations of underlying patterns and regularities. The clinician has a theory of personality functioning which guides him in progressively ordering and summarizing his observations, and the process of organizing the data begins from the moment the relationship is initiated between the investigator and his subject or patient. His underlying theory leads to a specification of which kinds of information should be collected, how this information should be collected, and what kinds of inferences and interpretations are appropriate for various purposes (20).

We, too, started with the observation of behavior, but no comprehensive theory was available for the interpretation of what we were to see. We were committed to studying the behavior of people who were not patients but who were working members of a business organization, functioning in a variety of situations. We had to effect some compromise between the study in depth of individual people and the study in depth of organizational structure and functioning. A review of the research literature and the comments of consultants suggested ideas for resolving these problems, but left us with the conclusion that no available theoretical scheme or method of analysis employed in previous studies would be wholly satisfactory. We knew, however, that we should strive to observe behavior in the actual work situation, and to take into account interpersonal and structural phenomena as well as individual attitudes and behaviors.

We resolved, then, to see as many people in as many different circumstances within the organization as we could, reasoning that the regularities in behavior and experience of people at work would be clarified by repeated encounters with numbers of people at numerous times by the various individual members of the research team. Our working principle in developing the sample was to have some contact with all of the work settings existing in any given location. We constructed a sample of the total roster of organization members, grouped by location, and, as circumstances in the field permitted, tried to see even more groups than had been included in the original sample. What this would mean in a specific community was as follows:

In one town, company personnel might include the division management and staff, office workers, the operating and maintenance crews at a local power plant, and the electric line and gas distribution field crews operating from a central warehouse, as well as personnel in meter shops and storerooms. With the cooperation of supervisors at each of these locations we had learned in advance the number of work groups into which these various people were organized and in which settings these group were located. On arriving in the community, we would spend as much time as was necessary to see at least one-third and preferably one-half of the total number in the work groups, taking care to have all of the major work locations represented. Sampling was more intensive at higher levels in the organization. All of top management and virtually all of the members of middle management were interviewed and many were observed on the job as well.

Once our working field plan had been developed we again visited each of the forty work locations for observation and interviews. Our practice was to spend up to a full day with a single group, getting acquainted with them by riding on the crew truck or visiting with them on the job, and later conducting individual interviews. These lasted from half an hour to an hour and one-half each. A day's field notes would consist of the transcriptions of individual interviews and a diary record of events during the day, including comments about interactions between the member of the research team and group members as well as features of the experience which suggested aspects of work life we had seen in other locations in the company. In these diary records, we included discussions within the research team about what had been learned in a given work location and tentative hunches that the individual researcher might have developed in the course of a day's field work experience. All of these field notes were transcribed as soon as possible after the actual field work for the day had been completed, usually the same evening.

Coverage of the company in this fashion took place over nearly two years. In the end, we had, as our recorded data, transcriptions of interviews with 874 members of the organization, a few of whom had been interviewed more than once by one or more team members. We had in addition several hundred pages of diary notes, and a large file of company publications, personnel rosters, background material on various communities, and historical materials from company files and newspaper records. Thus we now had some raw material of experience before us as well as our reflections about the meaning of that experience while we were going through it.

We had also made some progress in specifying more fully our conception of mental health. This particular advance came from the independent study conducted by two of us. We were aware — and our awareness was fortified in studies by others (16) — that attempts to define mental health ran the danger of being too abstract to be translated into researchable hypotheses and containing unrecognized assumptions about the nature of health, disease, and cure. Our decision was to adopt as operational and pragmatic a point of view as possible in resolving this problem. We decided to ask experienced observers on The Menninger Foundation's staff to describe for us people they had known whom they regarded to be mentally healthy. A large number of people were described. They differed widely in personal and social circumstances — old and young, native U.S. citizens and foreign-born, rural and urban dwellers, highly and minimally educated men and women. The clinicians who were doing the describing, had in common a psychoanalytic orientation, but they were of both sexes and differed considerably in age and place of training. An analysis of the interviews showed that certain features of behavior were mentioned very frequently by all of the interviewed clinicians in describing mentally healthy people. These aspects of behavior, referred to in chapter II, served as an operational definition of mental health.

These aspects of healthy functioning were so general that they could be applied in any life sphere. Our interest, of course, was the extent to which such descriptions of behavior would be useful in assessing mental health at work. We saw that each of the aspects of behavior identified as indicative of health could occur in work situations and might be affected by the conditions in the work setting confronted by a given person. For example, some jobs and some levels in an organization would involve people in a wider variety of ties to the environment than others. For some people in some situations, it would be likely that chances to learn about themselves and their capacities would be enhanced, whereas in other situations — perhaps highly routine work or work involving a limited number of responsibilities — this experience would be less likely. Similarly, understanding and acceptance of others as individuals would depend upon opportunities for engaging in interpersonal relationships, and work situations clearly varied in this respect. The stresses of work life were one class of stresses under which people might or might not be flexible. And, finally, some jobs offered a great likelihood that accomplishment — the experience of carrying through and completing an activity — would be a common experience.

Preliminary Reports

We knew that it would be a considerable period of time before we could complete the analysis of our data and produce a publishable report of our findings. Some months after the field work had been completed, word came to us both directly and indirectly that people at Midland wanted to hear about what progress we had made and what conclusions we had reached. This seemed to us not only a reasonable request but an obligation we had to assume. People in the organization had given us a great deal by sharing their work experiences with us. We wanted to return the favor by sharing our experience and preliminary results with them. It seemed desirable to do so even though we had as yet no "findings," and we had to abide by the terms of our relationship to the company as described in the Preface. Specifically, this prior agreement required that our observations about what we had learned would have to be stated in such a way that they could not be construed as diagnosis or advice concerning people or problem situations in the company.

While the interviews were relatively unstructured, we had in most instances opened our visits with individual employees with a few "priming" questions. These included: How did you happen to go to work at Midland? What makes a good supervisor? What kind of person do you prefer to work with? What would you change if you could about your work? What does your job involve? Whom do you see from other parts of the company? Not all these questions were asked in this way of everyone we saw, but most of the facets of work experience implied by them came up in every interview.

Thus we learned something of almost everyone's prior history in the company, what aspects of relationships to supervisors and peers were important to him, how he viewed the task he was assigned, and what was the nature of his contact with the larger organization. We developed empirically a set of categories to count the frequency of comments which had been made on each of these topics or subjects, and the range of opinions expressed on each. This enabled us to prepare a preliminary report for the people of Midland about what things had been discussed most often in their interviews, and to give some idea of the range of opinions expressed. In this way we were able to avoid relying solely on our impressions of interview *content* — we had some quantitative information. However our statistics were neither sufficient nor systematic so we did not offer them as evidence for conclusions.

While this work was going on we had completed the criterion study. The general aspects of behavior described as indicative of good mental health had been identified. These descriptions, too, became part of the report. We indicated the direction which our analysis would take by illustrating how varying work experiences could be seen in terms of these aspects of behavior (see appendix III).

By the conclusion of the field work we had both a wide range of experiences reported by people at Midland or observed by us in the course of the field work within the company. We had also a criterion applicable to the work situation. Our question then became: Under what conditions would these aspects of behavior be more likely to appear in work situations, and under what conditions would these behaviors be less likely to occur? We reasoned that these aspects of behavior would be possible to some degree for all people but that circumstances would vary and the work environment would influence the likelihood of any given aspect of experience or behavior occurring. Our clinical point of view led us to treat the behaviors and experiences of people in the company as *outcomes*, the result of the joint and interrelated effects of many processes, both within the person and in his environment, operating at the time of our study and in the past. Our task, then, was to identify and describe these underlying processes tending to enhance or inhibit behavior indicative of good mental health. We had to do this from the data we already had available which had been collected over as wide a range of work life in the company as we had been able to achieve. We would want to ask such questions as: Under what conditions, personal and organizational, are behaviors associated with positive mental health likely to occur? Conversely, what kinds of conditions, operating both within the person and within his work environment, seem to be accompanied by less evidence of healthy functioning? Our approach, in short, remained inductive. With the general perspective provided by the criterion study, we could review our data and begin to relate the regularities which we saw in the work experience of people within the company to the aspects of behavior associated with mental health.

Thematic Analysis

As we have already described in chapter II, our first step at this stage was to go back to the interview transcripts and diaries and to discover what features of experience had been most commonly reported or observed in the organization. We were less interested in identifying the particular circumstances and experiences of individual people in the organization than in locating the regularities which occurred for large numbers of people in many different kinds of work locations or at different kinds of work activities or at different levels within the company hierarchy. Yet we knew that the geographical distribution of Midland people in many plants and communities, and the many differences which existed between the work situations for various people within the company, required us to start at the local level in attempting this analysis. The process of thematic analysis, described in chapter II, was our approach to this problem.

The concepts which we ultimately evolved to account for these regularities — the interdependence of people with the organization, the problem of achieving optimal distance in interpersonal relations, the process of coping with change, the generally reciprocal character of relationships between person and organization — were arrived at by assessing the volume of evidence collected to discern patterns and regularities. The reader thus gets a view of the evolving conceptions which we gained with increasing experience.

This laborious process clearly involves more than, as one investigator has remarked, "immersing oneself in data and 'having insights'" (4). One has to be on guard constantly against importing ready-made theoretical assumptions or abstract concepts in organizing the data. For if this temptation is not resisted, the "analysis" becomes not a description of the relationships between various aspects of the phenomena studied, but the bare assertion of a principle and the illustration of that principle without resolving the question of proof.

ANNOUNCEMENT OF THE MIDLAND
STUDY IN EMPLOYEE PUBLICATION

WE ARE THE LEARNERS

By Harry Levinson, Director
Division of Industrial Mental Health
The Menninger Foundation

Work is one of the most important aspects of living. Not only do we spend nearly half of our waking hours at work, but what we do has very deep meaning for us.

Obviously, work provides our bread and butter, our homes, and our TV sets. But our work also brings us into contact with certain other people who may become friends and associates. Our work often determines where we live; we can only be a certain distance away from the job, and we live in houses and neighborhoods we can afford. Our conversations with our friends and neighbors frequently concern our work.

Work is our most direct tie with the world around us. Through our work we act on our environment and change it to meet our needs. For example, we create electricity, an event which completely changes how we live. Through our work also we earn our social places in our communities. We are known as linemen, engineers, secretaries, foremen or as whatever we do which makes a contribution to the total welfare of our friends and neighbors.

Work has much to do with how we feel about ourselves. During the depression of the '30's many men who couldn't find jobs felt completely useless as human beings. Some created little jobs around their homes just to be doing work — any kind of work. A man's work gives him a sense of being an adult, a sense of contributing to his fellow men.

Work is a key factor in knowing what goes on about us. In a few days of sickness at home or in the hospital we feel that we have been isolated and that we need to catch up on the news. Through association with others in our work we have contact with changing events —

we talk about the news in the papers, about baseball scores, about the drought, and we are in first-hand touch with what happens before our eyes. We can see the effects of lack of rain; we can ask each other how we are going to vote.

To have work is to have value to someone else. To have value to someone else is to be a necessary part of the scheme of living.

Work has an influence on many sides of our life. If we are unhappy in our work, this unhappiness has its effect on our home life. If we are happy with what we do and the people with whom we work, then this satisfaction contributes to more satisfying and richer living outside the work situation.

Despite the importance of work, very little effort has been made to study and understand just how someone's work influences his well-being. What specific factors in the work situation help make for greater satisfaction? What is it in his work that makes a fellow feel good about what he is doing? What is it about the relationships he has with other people on the job that gives him the feeling that this is a good gang to be with? How does his feeling about his work affect his feelings about his family, his home, his future?

There aren't many good answers to questions like these. We have much to learn.

Two and one-half years ago [1954] The Menninger Foundation became interested in these questions. Basically we were interested in what factors in our everyday lives keep people well and healthy. We had some ideas from our clinical experience about what makes people sick, but we had very little knowledge of what keeps them well. We felt that a very important factor in people's emotional health is their work.

We started out to learn about the circumstances under which people work and the kinds of problems which relate to work. We made a first-hand survey, visiting plants and industries from one coast to the other, traveling some 60,000 miles. From this look at American industry and from talking to hundreds of people, we developed what we believed to be a comprehensive picture of the many ways people work together under different circumstances. We learned something about the difficulties and problems of various businesses and industries. We developed some ideas for studying people at work and for learning from them what goes into good human relationships on the job.

The Rockefeller Brothers Fund thought this idea for studying in industry was worthwhile. They gave us a grant of $105,000 to develop a Division of Industrial Mental Health and to start our research. The next logical step was to find a company in which we could study. We had seen a cross section of people at work nationally. We needed to see a close-up intensively — a whole group of people working together in one organization. Several companies expressed their interest in our doing research in their plants. We ourselves decided on Midland and asked Midland to share in this study with us.

Why did we ask Midland? Yours is a company of long experience, of expansion and growth. You are recognized for the good service you give. You constantly face emergencies under the most difficult weather conditions and you go out and meet these emergencies successfully. Many different kinds of work groups, all coordinated, are needed to get this job done. And most important, the fact that you are able to grow, expand, give respected service, and meet extreme emergencies indicates that you have an ability to work together toward a common goal.

What has made for your joint success? What makes for your ability to work together under difficult circumstances? What are the important factors? If we could know them, then we would have learned something about that very vague term "human relationships."

Your chief executive officer has been closely interested in this project ever since we started. He agreed that Midland would collaborate in this research, but he emphasized that *nothing which was learned in the research was to affect in any way hiring, firing, promotions, demotions, wages, hours, or the on-going activities of the company.*

The research team, composed of Mr. Charlton Price and me (later there will be others), sees its relationship to Midland in this way. You have many long years of experience working together; we want to learn about it. You do a job; we want to observe what and how. You are the experts in this case; we are the learners.

This is a confidential arrangement. No person's name will be known to anybody but the researchers. All records and interviews will be kept confidential in a locked file at The Menninger Foundation. No information about the company, or any department or unit, will be given out, except in summarized, anonymous form as we report back to you, and with the permission of the company, to others.

This is not a consulting arrangement. We have not been called in by the company to deal with problems. We are not making recommendations for change. We are not part of management. Management does not pay us; we are supported by the Rockefeller grant. We are not passing judgment on the way anybody does his job. We are not concerned with merit rating, promotions, or training. We are not a part of any labor organization. Our sole concern is to learn.

So we will be visiting all parts of the company throughout its territory. We will be asking questions, having personal interviews with many of you ranging from the chairman of the board to the newest employee. Of course, since there are 2,000 of you, we won't be able to visit with all of you, but we do want you to know who we are and what we are doing in your organization. We want you to feel free to ask us questions when you see us.

When we learn something we think will be of interest to you, we'd like to report it to you. That may be some time off because research is a slow process, and sometimes you don't learn much for all your efforts. But we think we'll learn something and we'll want to share it with you.

We hope what we learn about human relations will be important to people everywhere, not just to you at Midland. We think we have a rare opportunity to contribute to science and to human welfare. We can't take advantage of this opportunity without your help. We hope, therefore, that when you see us coming around, you'll stick out your hand, introduce yourself, and try to teach us something about your job.

We'll be looking forward to meeting all of you.

ORAL REPORT TO MIDLAND EMPLOYEES

November 1958

WHEN the Menninger team started its study of Midland, we told you we would be back to report to you. Here we are. We haven't yet finished analyzing all of the information. We felt, however, that you would be interested in even a partial report now rather than waiting another year or so for the whole story.

What Have We Been Doing Since We Saw You Last?

The three members of the research team visited just about every Midland work location where there are five or more employees. There are more than 40 such places — division and local offices, power plants, compressor stations, and warehouses. We talked to 874, or more than a third, of the approximately 1950 people who were in the company at that time. The interviews averaged an hour each.

We did some other things as well. We rode with you on crew trucks in hot weather and cold, on ordinary days and during emergencies such as tornado alerts and line failures. We sat in offices, plants, and warehouses to get an idea of what your daily routine involves. We sat in on many meetings, ranging from the Monday morning meetings of the top staff in Shaw to tailgate conferences. In short, we tried to learn about life at Midland by having you tell us about it and by seeing it for ourselves.

Why Was This Done?

As we told you in the beginning, we wanted to learn how work and work experiences can help to keep well people well. What is there about work which can add to people's well-being and satisfaction in life? What is there about work which might have effects in the other direction? Here are some of the highlights of what you told us which start to answer these questions.

WHAT YOU HAVE

You and the Company

By and large, you have a deep sense of personal interest in your jobs and in the company. Some few, of course, view what they are doing as only a job, but for most others it is much more personal. Many of you have seen the company grow and change. You speak about improvements in equipment which have made the job easier. Many mentioned increasingly better wages, hours, and working conditions over the years.

Most of you talk of the security in this company. Even though layoffs and transfers may be made from time to time, you know the company is always going to be in business. Compared to the ups and downs of some other kinds of companies, Midland is relatively depression-proof. With pensions, sick benefits, insurance, and the company's policy of taking care of its own, you have some reasonable protection against the adversities of life. Many of you told us that the company treated you well when you were sick or injured. The forty-hour week is important to many, as is overtime opportunity. These things help you to have a sense of stability and order in your lives; you can make long-range plans and look ahead.

There is certainly, for many, a sense of reward in performing a unique, highly necessary job in your particular communities. You talk about the confidence other people in the community have in a Midland employee whom they regard to be reliable and stable because he works in the company. And beyond this there is the feeling that you want the company to prosper. Having cast your lot with Midland, its success is also your success. Many of you have bought stock in the company, which emphasizes this feeling.

You and the Job

Moving from the company to the job itself, there seem to be three major elements in satisfaction with work. So many of you spoke of the job as being a challenge, something to master, to overcome, to complete. Still others spoke of the variety of tasks in any given job and the sense of responsibility the job gives them. These things can keep a job from being routine.

Most impressive to us was the statement from many of you that you want to do a *good* job. You told us that you don't want to sit around doing nothing. You want to be busy doing something useful and constructive. After a day's work, you want to feel that you have made good use of your skills and of that time.

You express an interest in having a good place in which to work, one which is attractive to you and to the customer, one which speaks well for the company, and one which you can show off with pride to your friends.

You describe what a difference it makes to you when you have the tools and equipment that permit you to do your best work. As we watched some of you work, there were times when it seemed as if you had so much feeling for your tools and equipment that these were almost a part of you.

Supervisors and Fellow Workers

Almost everyone stressed the importance of good supervision and teamwork. You said that a good supervisor has to know his people and treat them fairly. Again and again this was emphasized. But you weren't asking for the supervisor to be just a good guy. You also wanted the supervisor to know the work and plan it well. And you said a good supervisor is one who keeps you informed on matters which affect you. You felt that a good supervisor has to be reliable, someone who will give you a straight answer, who treats everyone fairly, and who won't pass the buck.

When it came to the other people you work with, what you wanted most in the next person was sociability and friendliness. You pointed out that often the jobs that you do cannot be done by one person alone. As you work together, you come to depend very much on each other. You also noted that you are very sensitive to how the other person feels and are quickly affected by the next person's moods. But again, it wasn't enough for the next guy to be just a good guy. A good fellow worker is also one who will go out of his way to lend you a hand when that is necessary. You want to be able to rely on your fellow workers to take care of their own part of the job and you want the next person to be interested in doing a good job.

Of all the things you talked about with us, those having to do with supervision and with fellow workers were the most often mentioned. This is only natural. You spend half of your waking time with your friends at work. Often you depend on others for your very life. Even where danger is not a factor, your day-by-day feeling about yourself and your work depends very much on what the other people on the job think, feel, and do. You feel that good working relationships depend equally upon supervisors and fellow workers — not supervisors alone, not fellow workers alone, but both.

Self-Esteem

You stressed four things about your job which have to do with a feeling of self-esteem. These were pay, a feeling of independence, training, and communication. Discussion of pay was of two kinds. Some spoke about how much their pay would buy. Some compared their pay with wage and salary scales in their local area. It was clear from both kinds of comments that the matter of pay is of major importance in people's feelings of self-esteem.

Where you felt free to go ahead and do the job on your own, you spoke with pride about the satisfaction of doing the job well and the feeling that this gave you of being a mature adult.

Concerning training, you described how comfortable it felt to be taught to do a difficult job in the right way, to anticipate errors and dangers which might arise, to be able to master the tools and equipment with which you had to work and to be prepared for future changes. In other words, you looked upon training as an opportunity to learn and grow on the job.

You wanted to be informed about not only what was happening now in the company but what was likely to happen a little bit ahead. Especially you wanted others who were above you to know about you and how you felt. You wanted higher management to know what kinds of problems you were trying to deal with on the job.

WHAT YOU'D LIKE

I have talked much about the sources of satisfaction on the job that you told us about. But in any job or in any company, there are some things which may prevent people from getting as much satisfaction out of the job as they feel they could. You talked about these things, too.

Relations with the Company as a Whole

There is some regret that the company has grown bigger. You are glad to see increased demand for service. But, as a result, some of your ties with each other, and especially with people in higher management, are not as close or as personal as they used to be. Growth also has brought more formality, more "red tape," as you see it.

When someone from higher management comes by where you work and fails to take the time to visit, you lose an opportunity for personal contact. You feel that even though you know his time is limited it would mean a lot to you if he could stop by and visit with you.

You recognize the need for a chain of command and for rules and regulations to govern the work. However, when channels are not followed or when there is conflict between the supervisors above you, you report that this sometimes leaves you confused, not knowing who is boss or whose orders to follow.

You know that some things that happen on the job are not in keeping with company policy. You have often said to us that if top management knew about some of these things you are certain they would do something about them. Still you are sometimes left angry, frustrated, and irritated when there are conflicts up the line or you are not backed up in dealing with customers.

Efficiency and Economy

Because you want Midland to prosper, you want operations to be as efficient as possible. But some of you have mixed feelings about efficiency and economy. Many report that they can see many ways to economize but no one asks them for suggestions. In some cases you say you have suggested ways to save money but you were ignored. There are times when it seems to you shortsighted to save a few dollars now but spend more money later by undertaking a short-cut method, buying a less efficient piece of equipment, or arbitrarily cutting overtime.

You recognize there are emergencies when, despite the best laid plans, you will have to stop what you are doing and do something else. But you resent what appear to you to be some unnecessary changes in plans. Such changes, you feel, not only disrupt the sense of completion and satisfaction that you could get from a job but also sometimes force you to undo and repeat work which you have previously done.

When your equipment is not satisfactory, when you don't get the equipment you need or when it isn't kept in good shape, your pride in the job is less. This holds true for a shop or office. You feel that if you don't have the tools you need to do the job or your tools and equipment are in poor repair, the company must not consider your job very important.

Safety

Much is said about safety at Midland and many efforts are made to maintain a good safety record. But sometimes, you say, safety is talked about at 8 o'clock and forgotten at 9 o'clock when the boss starts pushing you to get something done. You said that when this happens, it makes it hard for a person to feel right about the job.

Fellow Workers

Regarding fellow workers, if you are in a group where someone looks down on you because you have less skill or less seniority than he, this can be a source of jealousy and resentment, because it interferes with good teamwork.

Self-Esteem

Now we come again to the four matters which have to do with the sense of self-esteem and which you mentioned so frequently: pay, a sense of independence, training, and communication.

This company includes a wide variety of jobs in many different locations over the state, and there is an equally wide variety of pay scales. Many people commented about this in the interviews, and there were many different opinions about how pay scales should be set up. A good many people simply said, "Everybody always wants more."

With respect to a feeling of independence, people said again and again, "I don't want anybody looking down my neck." A supervisor at whatever level who was "looking down the necks" of people below him made them feel as if they were unable to do the job, as if they were children instead of grown-ups. Naturally this produces considerable bad feeling where it occurs.

Independence and pride in job achievement are also reduced when those who make plans fail to have enough contact with those who have to do the jobs. This, you said, results at times in poor planning and errors. Both planners and people in the field are left feeling disappointed and angry.

A number of you feel that the company could do more about formal on-the-job training. Many said that the work is becoming too complex now to depend on a more traditional apprenticeship method for learning what you need to know. These people feel that if they were given more training, they would be more ready to meet coming changes and be of greater value to the company.

Some are content where they are and want no advancement, feeling they have all the responsibility they can handle. Others said they would like more information about chances for promotion than they now get. Many felt also that advancement should not be on the basis of seniority alone, that more consideration should also be given to individual merit.

Many people feel they are kept well informed about what is happening in the company through the employees' magazine, through the annual report, and through communications from their supervisors. But some say that even with the magazine and meetings, they learn most of what is going on in the company from the newspapers or customers. Some say that meetings are a waste of time because the subjects discussed aren't the things that people want and need to know about. Also, the feeling of many people was that everyone in the company would benefit from communication *up* the line as well as *down* the line.

The Union

Union members spoke frequently about the union. They felt that the more fully the union represented their views and spoke up for their interests the greater was its importance to them as individuals and to their relationship with management.

This, then, is a very quick summary of the things about working at Midland which most of you mentioned most often.

MENTAL HEALTH

What Does All This Have to Do with "Mental Health"?

To get an answer to this question required that we do a separate study outside Midland while we were working in the company. The purpose of this outside study was to come up with a definition of mental health which would make scientific sense and also practical sense on the job. We asked fifteen senior doctors on The Menninger Foundation staff to describe for us the most mentally healthy people they had known. They described for us many different kinds of people they knew: men and women, old and young, rich and poor, native Americans and foreign-born. Despite all these differences in healthy people who were described, *the behavior of each one was discussed in much the same way, often with the same words.* The descriptions given boiled down to four key statements, which can be thought of as four principles of healthy behavior. I'll mention each principle and then tell you how we think it helps us to understand better the things we learned from you about your job experience.

Principle 1. A mentally healthy person has many different sources of satisfaction in his life.

A tree with many roots is stronger than one with few roots. So it is with a man. The more ties he has to the world around him, the more sources of satisfaction he has available.

What are some possible sources of satisfaction at Midland?

Certainly there is a wide variety of ways to get satisfaction in your work. You yourself spelled them out for us. To recall just a few: security in the company, job variety, usefulness to your community, and the sense of challenge and of completion. And then you described some of the things which make it more difficult to get some of the satisfactions which you might otherwise have: losing personal contact with management as the company grows larger, differences of opinion about pay, preventable interruptions on the job, supervisors who won't let you have a say, or fellow workers who won't do their share.

Principle 2. A mentally healthy person is flexible under stress.

All of us face stresses of various kinds as long as we're alive. The key question is: How well can we deal with stress? To come back to the example of the tree, if a tree can bend with the storm it has a much better chance of coming through the storm unbroken than a tree which is more rigid and brittle. For people, flexibility under stress means the ability to "bounce back" and keep on going when things get rough.

How can job conditions help make it possible to be more flexible?

You mentioned freedom to do the job in your own way, adequate training, and safe working conditions as some aspects of the job which back you up when things get tough. You said it helps to have a change of pace. If the pressure eases up once in awhile, then a person can cope more effectively with an emergency if it does come. But if your bosses are in disagreement, if your immediate supervisor is always telling you every step to take, or if you are not sure what is the right thing to do in the company's eyes, then it is difficult for you to act quickly and wisely when stress or pressure occurs.

Principle 3. A mentally healthy person recognizes and accepts his own limits.

Each of us has certain skills and talents, a certain amount of education, and a certain personality. We try to use these in our own best interests. To do so requires a pretty good look at ourselves and a frank recognition of what we see there. A person cannot be mentally healthy if he tries to do or be something which makes him untrue to his real nature. A man is both wise and healthy if he knows himself and is content with trying to become all that is possible for *him*.

What is there about a job which can help people to do this?

The range of jobs available in this company gives many people a chance to try out different kinds of work. This makes it possible to learn what a person can or cannot do, what he likes and what he doesn't like. Many an employee says he doesn't want to be a lineman; that's too dangerous. Frequently linemen say they've tried working inside and they don't like it. Others will say they've tried being acting foremen and they don't like that. The stability of the company also gives a person a pretty good idea of where he might be able to go from where he is and what the possibilities are. He can size up himself and the jobs which are open to him and gauge his own limits and assets in a realistic way. For some, of course, limits have not yet been reached. Because training or opportunities for exploring a variety of jobs have not been made available, it is more difficult for some to know what is or is not possible for them.

Principle 4. A mentally healthy person accepts others as individuals.

That is, he shows understanding of and respect for other people as human beings who are different from each other and from him, who have strengths, and weaknesses, needs and problems just as he does.

What things about the company make it possible to accept others as individuals?

Many people in the company have received special consideration when they were ill, had family troubles, or were hurt. People who have no longer been able to continue on their old jobs have been moved to others which they could do. But when one is not shown consideration himself, as when a supervisor fails to give a person a chance to speak up, or when favoritism is shown to some people, or when people are treated as if they were less important than the machines with which they work, it is hard for this fourth principle to operate. [The fifth principle was left out in this presentation because discussions about whether it should be listed separately were still going on within the team.]

SUMMARY

People at Midland want stability and security, opportunity to be of service to other people, respect and responsibility in the community, fair-minded supervision, and friendly working relationships with others on the job. These are things which you say are most important to your own mental health. By and large, what you find at Midland comes close to what you say you need and what you expect. This is not to say that everyone is a model of mental health — no one is perfect in that sense. It is not to say that everyone finds equal opportunity in his job to fulfill all four of the mental health principles. It *is* to say that you find in your work and in your company many possible encouragements to mentally healthy behavior, together with opportunities for developing even more.

IN CONCLUSION

Certainly these are not all of the things that you talked about nor does this brief summary represent even a major part of our study. If we had more time together, it would be possible to go into greater detail on just about every point I have mentioned.

You will understand, of course, that we have discussed this report with management before bringing it to you. What we are presenting, however, are our own conclusions, and we assume full responsibility for them.

Much of what you have heard in this report may seem like old stuff.

You live with it every day. But if you were to compare yourselves with people who work in a different kind of industry, such as an automobile assembly plant or an airplane plant, you would see some sharp differences. People doing other kinds of work in other organizations will have very different opinions about their relationships to their companies and their fellow workers. So this study of Midland gives us only one picture in one kind of business. We won't have learned all we can until we have compared our research on Midland with what we hope to learn in other companies.

What may seem obvious to you may still be highly important to science. Remember, we said we wanted to know about *your experiences,* how you saw things and how you felt about them. We think we have learned a great deal from our visits with you. We think, also, that others will be interested in learning from your experiences in this company. That's why we will publish our study in book form.

Some of you may feel that we think everything at Midland is rosy. We don't. There are problems at Midland, as there are in any other company, and we have touched on some of them in a general way. It was not our purpose to make a list of problems, one by one. Nor was it our purpose to whitewash anyone or shake anyone up. All we have tried to do is to get a picture of work at Midland and to relate this to mental health. Our report, therefore, does not represent the way some individuals feel. But since we have summarized the feelings of 874 people across the state, we can give you a more complete picture than you would have if we had reported the feelings of any single one of the people we interviewed.

We are still working on the interviews. We hope to be finished with all of them and to have a rough draft of our complete report ready by the end of the year. Then it will take us several months to put it in book form. When that's done, we'll let you know about it through your magazine so that those of you who want to read the book may do so.

We hope that even these few highlights from the research will offer you some idea of what your fellow employees expect from you, whether you be on the line, in the office, a foreman, a supervisor, a manager, or someone in top management. We hope you will think more about how your job experience relates to the four principles of good mental health.

HOW YOU HELPED

In the beginning I said that this brief report is our one chance to repay you in a small way for all the help you have given us. By letting us come into the company, talk with you, and be with you on the job, you helped us in three very specific ways:

a. You gave us the chance to learn how to study a whole organization at once. We will now go on and study other companies.

b. All of these "results" I have been giving you are really only questions, which have to be checked out in future research with other companies. What you have done for us is to help us learn which questions are *worth* asking.

c. In both these ways, your cooperation and help will some day mean better mental health for people everywhere. You helped those of us in mental health work to start down the road toward that objective which everyone would like to see come true.

For all of this, we can't repay you. We can only say: Thank you — it's been great to get to know you.

[Following this report, the employees were invited to ask the reporter any questions they wished. This permitted elaboration and explanation to the satisfaction of the listeners.]

REFERENCES

1. Argyris, C., "Human Relations in a Bank," *Harvard Business Review*, 32:63–72 (September–October 1954).
2. ——, *Personality and Organization* (New York: Harper, 1957).
3. Bakke, E. W., *The Fusion Process* (New Haven: Yale Labor and Management Center, 1955).
4. Becker, H. S., "Problems of Inference and Proof in Participant Observation," *American Sociological Review*, 23:652–660 (December 1958).
5. Bell, D., *Work and Its Discontents* (Boston: Beacon, 1956).
6. Bennis, W. G., "Leadership Theory and Administrative Behavior: The Problem of Authority," *Administrative Science Quarterly*, 4:259–301 (December 1959).
7. Clarke, A. C., "The Use of Leisure and Its Relation to Levels of Occupational Prestige," *American Sociological Review*, 21:301–307 (June 1956).
8. Dubin, R., "Industrial Workers' Worlds: A Study of the Central Life Interests of Industrial Workers," *Social Problems*, 3:131–142 (January 1955).
9. Fiedler, F. E., *Leader Attitudes and Group Effectiveness* (Urbana: University of Illinois, 1958).
10. Freud, S., *Complete Psychological Works* (London: Hogarth, 1955) XVIII, 101.
11. Gouldner, A. W., "Cosmopolitans and Locals: Toward an Analysis of Latent Social Roles, I," *Administrative Science Quarterly*, 2:281–306 (December 1957).
12. ——, "The Norm of Reciprocity: A Preliminary Statement," *American Sociological Review*, 25:161–178 (April 1960).
13. Grinker, R., ed., *Toward a Unified Theory of Human Behavior* (New York: Basic Books, 1956).
14. Gurin, G., J. Veroff, and S. Feld, *Americans View Their Mental Health: A Nationwide Interview Survey* (New York: Basic Books, 1960).
15. Halliday, J., *Psychosocial Medicine* (New York: Norton, 1948).
16. Jahoda, M., *Current Concepts of Positive Mental Health* (New York: Basic Books, 1958).
17. Jaques, E., *The Changing Culture of a Factory* (New York: Dryden, 1952).

18. Katz, D., N. Maccoby, and N. Morse, *Productivity, Supervision and Morale in an Office Situation: Part I* (Ann Arbor, Michigan: Institute for Social Research, Monograph Series 2, 1950).
19. Leighton, A. H., J. A. Clausen, and R. N. Wilson, eds., *Explorations in Social Psychiatry* (New York: Basic Books, 1957).
20. Lippitt, R., J. Watson, and B. Westley, *The Dynamics of Planned Change: A Comparative Study of Principles and Techniques* (New York: Harcourt, 1958).
21. Lundberg, G. A., M. Komarovsky, and M. A. McInerny, *Leisure: A Suburban Study* (New York: Columbia, 1934).
22. Mann, F. C., and L. R. Hoffman, *Automation and the Worker* (New York: Holt, 1960).
23. McGregor, D., *The Human Side of Enterprise* (New York: McGraw-Hill, 1960).
24. McLean, A. A., and G. C. Taylor, *Mental Health in Industry* (New York: McGraw-Hill, 1958).
25. Menninger, K. A., *Theory of Psychoanalytic Technique* (New York: Basic Books, 1958).
26. Menninger, W. C., *Psychiatry in a Troubled World* (New York: Macmillan, 1948).
27. ———, and H. Levinson, "Industrial Mental Health: Some Observations and Trends," *Menninger Quarterly*, 8:1–13 (Fall, 1954).
28. Sayles, L. R., *Behavior of Industrial Work Groups* (New York: Wiley, 1958).
29. Schutz, W. C., *FIRO: A Three Dimensional Theory of Interpersonal Behavior* (New York: Rinehart, 1958).
30. Seeley, J. R., R. A. Sim, and E. Loosley, *Crestwood Heights* (New York: Basic Books, 1956).
31. Smith, M. B., "Mental Health Reconsidered: A Special Case of the Problem of Values in Psychology," *American Psychologist*, 16:299–306 (June 1961).
32. Solley, C. M., and K. J. Munden, "Toward a Description of Mental Health," *Bulletin of The Menninger Clinic*, 26:178–188 (July 1962).
33. Spitz, R. A., "Hospitalism," in *Psychoanalytic Study of the Child*, I, 53–74 (1945).
34. Whyte, W. F., *Man and Organization* (Homewood, Illinois: Irwin, 1959).

INDEX

Absenteeism, 168
Accidents, 56, 70
Administration techniques, 11
Affection, 66, 74, 76, 101
Age: changes with, 93; dependency needs and, 45; Elders, 82, 85, 88, 90, 105, 164; performance and, 81
Aggression, 56, 149
Anger: changes and, 95, 104; displacement of, 118; dual instincts and, 77; leader loss and, 99; toward new boss, 62; withdrawal and, 66; worker and, 42
Anthropologist, 173
Anxiety, 73
Argyris, Chris, 13, 37, 43
Atomic energy, 81
Attitude: free enterprise, 35; toward work, 23
Authority: dependency needs of, 55; company and, 25, 55; father figure, 69; patterns of, 49; relations to, 43, 48, 50, 54, 56, 75; work environment and, 9
Authority figures: attitudes, 147; dependency needs and, 50; distance from, 140; identification with, 60, 130, 165; lack of, 41; manager and, 95; workers and, 9, 137
Automation, 11, 80, 102
Autonomy: dependency needs and, 44; top management, 11

Bakke, E. Wight, 20
Behavior: of company, 40, 109; dependency needs and, 85; in emergency, 124; goals and, 10; group, 14; mental health characteristics in, 18; social process and, 59, 63, 66, 78, 106, 174; under stress, 76, 124, 149, 162; of supervisor, 70, 77; of worker, 14, 130, 167
Bell, Daniel, 111
Bennis, Warren, 70

Boy Scouts, 114
Business: See *Company*

Centrality, 111
Citizenship of workers, 34
Clausen, J. A., 173
Clinical psychologist, 16
Coffee break, 73
Collins, Ralph, 171
Communication: of complaints, 53; failure in, 42; and isolation, 73; Midland workers and, 192
Community: company and, 10, 93, 108, 151; identification with, 94; management and, 8, 91; public utility and, 10, 34
Company: benefits in, 188; changes, 81, 89, 100, 154, 157, 170; community and, 10, 93, 108; conflict resolution, 130, 152; consultants, 171; expansion, 10; expectations, 96; exploitation of, 134; goals, 142, 160; holding, 9; interdependence, 32; merger, 132; partnership with worker, 154, 160; permissiveness of, 112; personality of, 10; policies, 48; as protector, 30; reputation of, 108; security and, 48, 84; separation from, 94; sick benefits, 128; status in, 148; structure, 48; value system, 154
Compensation, 120, 166
Competition, job security and, 31
Complementarity, 113
Conant, James, 171
Confidential material, 185
Conflict: organization, 144, 146; overcompensation and, 166; reciprocation and, 155; resolution of, 130, 141, 152, 157, 161, 165
Contract: See *Psychological contract*
Coping: See *Stress*
Cosmopolitans, 25, 33
Counseling, marriage, 173